2-15-2019

FOR ~~EDR~~ ~~PAT~~
SHANNON
~~CHRISTINE~~

--- DAD

(OR MARTY IS ALSO)
FINE

Praise for *Pendulum*

"How do you predict what kind of society we're in? How do you know when's the right time to make a difference? In *Pendulum*, Roy H. Williams and Michael R. Drew have combed through history's ups and downs and the cultural shifts that ripple through every generation. They've written a unique guidebook that has an interesting perspective for marketers, entrepreneurs, and anyone who is thinking about how to live in the now—and in the future."

—**Tony Hsieh,** *New York Times* **Best-selling Author of**
Delivering Happiness, **and CEO of Zappos.com**

"*The Pendulum* offers fascinating insights into the surprises and revelations of shifting social trends throughout history. Roy H. Williams and Michael R. Drew answer the age-old question: What makes us tick?"

—**Harvey Mackay, Author of the #1** *New York Times* **Best Seller,**
Swim With The Sharks Without Being Eaten Alive

How about the following...

"Understanding how civilization shifts its mindset on a decadal level is critical to business and governance. In *Pendulum*, Michael R. Drew and Roy H. Williams have synthesized several thousand years of history and figured out why we've acted the way we do. Better yet, they've also given us a road map of what it means going forward. This is a great tool to understand and even predict business and social trends."

— **Peter H. Diamandis, Founder and Chairman of the X PRIZE Foundation, Executive Chairman**
of Singularity University, New York Times Best-selling Author of *Abundance*

"We're bombarded by so much information that sometimes we don't know which way is up. And when it comes to the world around us, it's tough to see how civilization works. But *Pendulum* shows you how to take advantage of cultural moods, societal shifts and generational swings—all thanks to the research that Michael R. Drew and Roy H. Williams have done. They've combed through 3,000 years of history and found the key to what makes us tick. What's more, they show how you can benefit from it, whether you're a financial analyst, a marketing whiz or a consumer who wants to understand the world a little better."

—David L. Bach, Founder of FinishRich.com and Author of *The Automatic Millionaire,*
Smart Women Finish Rich, and many other best sellers

"Of the many people with whom I've worked, I've met few as authentic and brilliant as Michael R. Drew and Roy H. Williams. Now, after reading *Pendulum*, I've come to see why people think the way they do and how they'll think in the future. Thanks to the behavioral insights *Pendulum* showed me, I've discovered how the average person thinks, and I've learned why my old ways of speaking weren't getting through. I've made changes in my presentations as a speaker and comedian, and everything has changed. Once you see how *Pendulum* works, you can adjust to everything. If you, like me, are the type of person who needs proof of everything, you'll find it with *Pendulum*."

—Kyle Cease, Voted #1 Comedian on Comedy Central for 2009

"In *Pendulum,* Roy H. Williams and Michael R. Drew take us through a revealing inquiry that challenges our assumptions about the potential of patterns in life and business. This is a thought-provoking book you will be glad you read; it stretches your thinking regardless of your generation or professional expertise. *Pendulum* is a powerful, out-of-the-box message that will forever shift your perspective and dramatically inform your influence. Read it before your competition does."

—Greg Link, Co-founder of CoveyLink and Co-author of
Smart Trust: Creating, Prosperity, Energy, and Joy in a Low-Trust World

"My thoughts about this book are swinging like a pendulum—from stunningly visionary to intensely practical, from wildly theoretical to staggeringly personal. Read *Pendulum* to find out why you became who you are today . . . and why you'll become the person you'll become tomorrow. Kudos to Williams and Drew!"

—Robert G. Allen, Author of the *New York Times* Best Sellers,
Creating Wealth, Multiple Streams of Income and *The One Minute Millionaire*

"In today's business environment, you need to anticipate and understand consumers as never before. You need to drive change and create step-and-repeat processes. Roy H. Williams and Michael R. Drew nail it in *Pendulum*. They've looked in the mirror of history, and found a reflective pattern. And while every businessperson is running the gauntlet of business, they can use the book to become more competitive, nimble and ready to drive change and grow! Every generation thinks a bit differently than the previous one—and *Pendulum* tells you why. Saddle up for an insightful read, and an essential tool."

— **Jeffrey Hayzlett, Former CMO Kodak, Global Business & Marketing Authority, and Best-selling Author of** *The Mirror Test* **and** *Running the Gauntlet*

"Hindsight gives you 20/20 vision. What if you had 20/20 foresight vision? What if you knew exactly what people were thinking and what they wanted to buy? Would that help you make more money? Then read *Pendulum* . . . before your competition does."

—**Darren Hardy, Publisher,** *SUCCESS magazine* **and** *New York Times* **Best-selling Author of** *The Compound Effect*

"If you want to better understand the world we live in, then read *Pendulum*. Roy H. Williams and Michael R. Drew have uncovered the secrets to how society shifts from generation to generation—and why that matters to all of us. I've devoted my career to helping people experience greater happiness, and this book has given me more tools that support personal breakthroughs."

—**Ivan Misner, Ph.D.,** *New York Times* **Best-selling Author and Founder of BNI®**

"In *Pendulum*, Roy H. Williams and Michael R. Drew show us that society rises and falls not only on the strength of its leaders, but also through the generational context in which they find themselves."

—**Geoff Smart and Randy Street,** *New York Times* **Best-selling Authors of** *Who: The A Method for Hiring*

"Everyone wants to predict the future, but Michael R. Drew and Roy H. Williams have actually done it by analyzing the past. *Pendulum* explores the generational shifts of the last 3,000 years to help us understand what's in store for us. Using cultural milestones, historical events and even biblical stories, they show how society shifts every 40 years or so, and how marketers today can be much more effective. For anyone who wants a business to survive and grow in the next decades, it's essential to understand the swings of history. *Pendulum* does just that. It's enlightening, insightful and just a little scary."

—**Marshall Goldsmith, Million-selling Author of** *New York Times* **Best Sellers** *MOJO* **and** *What Got You Here Won't Get You There*

"Most of us want to find patterns in our lives and to glimpse into the future. *Pendulum* offers an innovative and creative way to do both. Societies clearly shift over time from a focus on Me to We and back again. When we recognize societal trends, we can make better business and personal choices to respond to these shifts."

— **Dave Ulrich**, *New York Times* **Best-selling author of** *The Why of Work,* **Professor, Ross School of Business, University of Michigan, Partner, the RBL Group (www.rbl.net)**

"Reading *Pendulum* is like having a master class in social theory, cultural history and target marketing. Roy H. Williams and Michael R. Drew have given us a blueprint for speaking to today's consumer and tomorrow's customer. You'll be amazed by what you can learn from these guys, and how you can use what they've discovered about what makes us all tick."

— **Loral Langemeier, Four-time** *New York Times* **Best-selling Author**

"Roy H. Williams and Michael R. Drew have gone through almost all of western history and found out how each of us looks at the world—and how it changes over time. So much of today's marketing doesn't work because people don't know *why* we make the decisions we do, or what appeals to us. Roy and Michael know. They discovered the reasons we work together at one point while at others we act on our own. And why knowing that is indispensable for anyone in business. I've told everyone about these remarkable concepts, but now you can explore them yourself. *Pendulum* is enlightening, entertaining, essential reading."

—**Marci Shimoff,** *New York Times* **Best-selling Author,** *Happy for No Reason*

"If you've ever wondered why people did what they did, why cultural change happened and even what led to some of mankind's greatest discoveries, then *Pendulum* has the answers. Roy H. Williams and Michael R. Drew take you through three millennia on an astounding roller-coaster ride of shifts in society to get at the heart of why we do what we do—and how we can understand not only where we are, but where we're going."

—**Greg S. Reid, Co-author of** *Think and Grow Rich: Three Feet from Gold*

"In business, fortunes are made from predicting and riding trends in the marketplace. Match your product or message to the current trend and you look like a genius. Match it to a declining one and it could cost you everything. *Pendulum* tells you when and why and how these trends have occured in the past, when they're likely to occur in the future and how you can position your products and services to match what the market really wants (even before the market knows what it wants). *Pendulum* is the closest thing to a crystal ball that any business owner, manager or decision-maker will ever encounter."

—**Ryan Deiss, Internet marketing expert, Founder/President at Infomastery LLC**

"Michael and Roy have nailed it! If you want to know where the future is headed and prepare for what is to come, then you have to read this book. *Pendulum* will help you better understand society and social behavior like it has never before been explained. This book is a true gem and a must-read."

—**Randy Garn, CRO of Prosper Inc., and the author of *New York Times***
Best-seller, *Prosper: Create the Life You Really Want*

"Roy H. Williams and Michael R. Drew have taken centuries of civilization and made sense of its ups and downs. They've distilled 3,000 years of history and figured out why we've ridden a roller coaster from outward thinking to inner leaning every 40 years. Thanks to their insights, every businessperson, marketer, networker, and entrepreneur will be armed with the knowledge and tools to make the best of wherever society takes us as we move into the future."

—**Garrett B. Gunderson, *New York Times* Best-selling Author of *Killing Sacred Cows***

"Everyone wants to know the future, but only Roy H. Williams and Michael R. Drew have figured out how to predict it by examining the past. In their new book, *Pendulum,* they explore how society has shifted every generation throughout 3,000 years of history and uncovered essential insights that will help any marketer, any communicator, understand the world and how to reach customers."

—**Peggy McColl, *New York Times* Best Selling Author of *Your Destiny Switch***

"If you want to know why you're in sync or out of it with what's going on in the world, you must read *Pendulum*. This is a book that lays out what society's going through, and how it changes back and forth over time. *Pendulum* is the kind of book you put down and want to pick up again—it's got so many insights into how we act, feel and see."

—**Cathy L. Greenberg, Funder of excelinstitute.com and Co-author of the Best-selling Books,**
***What Happy Companies Know* and *What Happy Women Know,* among others**

"If you want to make it big, you dream big—but you've got to know the big picture. *Pendulum* gives you that and more. It's filled with dazzling insights into how society works on the deepest level and how that will affect your marketing, and your outlook."

—**Vince Poscente, Former Olympic Competitor,** *New York Times* **Best-selling Author,** *The Age of Speed: Learning to Thrive in a More-Faster-Now World* **and other books**

"Successful entrepreneurs, investors, artists and advertisers are dialed into a frequency the rest haven't yet found. They tap emerging trends and tastes with crystal-ball-like accuracy. With *Pendulum*, Roy H. Williams and Michael R. Drew offer the rest of us a simple paradigm for understanding how people and their preferences predictably change in generational cycles. It's an essential blueprint for anyone who wants to know how to look at markets and understand today's culture."

— **Jay Papasan,** *New York Times* **Best-selling Author of** *The Millionaire Real Estate Investor*

"*Pendulum* is a profoundly powerful read. This revelatory new book provides insight to social trends that will emerge in the years to come. *Pendulum* impacted how I approach business and it will change how you view the world."

—**Rich Christiansen, Entrepreneur and Author of the** *USA Today* **Best-selling Book,** *The Zig Zag Principle*

"To flourish, organizational leaders need to identify the challenges and opportunities in the greater world. In their insightful book, *Pendulum,* Roy H. Williams and Michael R. Drew provide new lenses that clarify societal shifts and trends so leaders can thrive."

—**Dennis A. Romig, PhD, CEO, and Author of** *New York Times* **Best Seller,** *Side by Side Leadership*

"Times change, but some things remain consistent: People either think of themselves or of others. The question is, how do you know when (and what does it mean)? Roy H. Williams and Michael R. Drew have figured that out in *Pendulum*, their razor-sharp look at cultural shifts over the last 3,000 years (and the next ones too). Whether you try to come up with a new dish at KFC, a special pie at Pizza Hut or a menu change at Taco Bell, you need to know your customer. *Pendulum* gives you that knowledge."

—**Jonathan Blum, SVP and Chief Public Affairs and Global Nutrition Officer of YUM! Brands**

(Praise for Pendulum *continued at the end of the book)*

Pendulum

Pendulum

How Past Generations Shape Our Present
and Predict Our Future

Roy H. Williams and Michael R. Drew

Vanguard Press
A Member of the Perseus Books Group

New York

Published by Vanguard Press
A Member of the Perseus Books Group

Cover Design: Leigh Jeffrey
Editorial production by *Marra*thon Production Services. www.marrathon.net
Designed by Hespenheide Design
Set in 11.5/14 point Minion Pro Regular

Cataloging-in-Publication data for this book is available from the Library of Congress.

ISBN: 978-1-59315-706-7 (hardcover)
ISBN: 978-1-59315-715-9 (e-Book)

Vanguard Press books are available at special discounts for bulk purchases in the U.S. by corporations, institutions, and other organizations. For more information, please contact the Special Markets Department at the Perseus Books Group, 2300 Chestnut Street, Suite 200, Philadelphia, PA 19103, or call (800) 810-4145, ext. 5000, or e-mail special.markets@perseusbooks.com.

10 9 8 7 6 5 4 3 2 1

Contents

Preface

If you will see into the heart of a people, look closely at what they create. Examine the inventions to which they pay the most attention. Read their best-selling books. Listen to their popular music. This is how you will know them.

—*Roy H. Williams*

Having made my ninety-minute presentation on "Society's Forty-Year Pendulum" to over 240 auditoriums full of people in the past eight years, I began this book by trying to disprove my own "forty-year" hypothesis.

My friend, Dr. Kary Mullis, winner of the 1993 Nobel Prize in Chemistry, said,

> Roy, there are few true scientists left in the world. Too often a scientist will develop a hypothesis and then look for supporting evidence. They identify with their hypothesis, and they want it to be correct. This is bad science. When you have a hypothesis, your job is to try to disprove it. No one knows more about your hypothesis than you do. No one else is as qualified to discover its flaws. When you believe a thing to be true, your first responsibility is to do everything you can to disprove it.

As I attacked my hypothesis to disprove it, I found three major loopholes:

1. I had chosen the examples in my presentation *after* I developed my theory.

2. My presentation was US-centric. I was using the *Billboard* charts to follow patterns in music and the *New York Times* Best Sellers List to follow patterns in literature.

3. All my examples came from the past 120 years. My original motive in this was that my audience needed to be familiar with the events. But if my forty-year hypothesis was true, it should be observable in any century.

With Kary's voice ringing in my head, I decided to:

A. throw out all the familiar data in my ninety-minute presentation;

B. begin a new investigation using completely new data, whose patterns and connections I would have no way of knowing in advance;

C. gather this new data from persons who had never seen my presentation;

D. use the international hit-tracking website TsorT instead of *Billboard*;

E. use the *Publishers Weekly* list instead of the *New York Times*;

F. examine every forty-year window in the past three thousand years; and

G. use a single source, Wikipedia, for establishing the dates of events in question.

This book is the result of that investigation.

Note: The careful reader will notice a number of sentence fragments, lists and short passages taken directly from Wikipedia and TsorT. The authors wish to acknowledge our debt to the worldwide teams of unnamed experts who have graciously contributed their time and expertise to these marvelous online endeavors. Thank you.

Due to the fact that each of these databases is updated daily with new information, it is inevitable that some of the dates will change and the song rankings will be altered. When this occurs, we hope you will retest our hypothesis against the new facts as they are presented and judge for yourself whether our thesis remains reliable.

—*Roy H. Williams and Michael R. Drew*

Introduction

The key to riding the waves is to understand the forces that move the masses and know approximately when a society will reverse and head back the other direction.
—Michael R. Drew

You've seen the public redefine what is acceptable and what is not. But by what process do we choose the new rules? It feels as though the earth is shifting beneath our feet.

Having made my living for thirty years as an advertising consultant to small business owners nationwide, I've heard thousands of them practically sing in chorus, "Ads that worked well in the past aren't working anymore. What should we do now? What happens next? Where do we go from here?"

The questions I needed to answer for them were: *What are the forces that drive the decisions of the public? What makes people do the things they do?*

Journey with Michael R. Drew and me as we examine the predictable, rhythmic attractions that move a society from one extreme to another. Together we'll examine where we've been and how we got there. When we get back to where we started, you'll know where society is headed and understand the forces that move us like flotsam on the tide. You'll know exactly how to get in step with the public's expectations.

Not only that, you'll be able to stay a step ahead of them. The new rules of success will be clear to you.

Predictable, rhythmic attractions are what move our society. Rhythm is intrinsic to the human experience. Feet patter, hearts beat, lungs breathe, planets circle, and seasons cycle to a rhythm. Music, poetry, and dance are built upon it.

The yearnings of the heart are cyclical as well. We are rhythmically pulled toward one hunger and away from another. Back and forth we travel, forever dissatisfied, because the hardest choices in life are those that are between two good things. But we don't move between these poles as individuals; we move collectively, as a society.

Solomon observed these endless cycles three thousand years ago and wrote,

> What has been will be again, what has been done will be done again; there is nothing new under the sun. Is there anything of which one can say, 'Look! This is something new'? It was here already, long ago; it was here before our time. No one remembers the former generations, and even those yet to come will not be remembered by those who follow them.
>
> —*Ecclesiastes 1:9–11*

As you read this book, you'll recall those words of Solomon and think, *How very right he was!* If only we could learn to examine the experiences of former generations, perhaps we could learn how to avoid taking good things too far.

How to Read This Book

To get the most out of this book, we've added images and charts that will help you apply and understand the we are going to share with you.

Pendulum takes you back in time through the last 3,000 years of history to explore how the 40-year shifts in society have affected Western society.

Your Roadmap to the Pendulum Cycle

Throughout this book, these graphics will show you visually where you are in the Pendulum cycle as we transition back and forth from a "ME" cycle to a "WE" cycle.

The text and graphics that are in orange indicate that you are reading about events during a "ME" cycle.

Figure 1.1 "ME" cycle.

Green text and graphics indicate a "WE" cycle.

Figure 1.2 "WE" cycle.

Pendulum Legend

Search for a Rosetta Stone that will give you a window into the minds
of these barbarians at the gate, so that in the future at least you'll know
how to do business with them.

CHAPTER ONE

Epiphany

"Nick, we just finished 1963 all over again, but this time we're headed in the opposite direction."

"What do you mean, exactly?"

It was late November, 2003. I was talking to my friend Dr. Richard D. Grant, a psychologist and teacher of Consumer Behavior in the MBA program at the University of Texas in Austin. Like many people, I ponder the events of the year each autumn and try to make sense of it all. In the fall of 2003, I had a nagging sense of déjà vu.

In 1991, twelve years prior to my strange "1963 all over again" proclamation, I had read *The Popcorn Report*, in which Faith Popcorn suggested, "A trend is a fad that lasts at least ten years." As those next ten years progressed, the accuracy of her predictions continued to amaze me.

Faith Popcorn's forecasts evolved exactly as she said they would. When you read *The Popcorn Report* today, her predictions seem fairly obvious. This is due to what Harvard Business School calls "The Curse of Knowledge"—*you can't imagine not knowing what you know.* But if you had read that book in 1991 as I did, those predictions were gutsy, audacious, and profoundly insightful.

In one of her closing chapters, Ms. Popcorn very presciently describes what we now know as e-mail and e-commerce, though she called them *ScreenMail* and *InfoBuying,* even though neither had yet been invented. When she coined those words, the average American was completely unaware of connectivity. *World Wide Web* and *Internet* were terms that were not yet in the common lexicon. It would

be another two years before the average person would begin hearing rumblings about a soon-to-come "Information Superhighway."[1] Even the most forward-thinking technologists weren't anticipating search engines. In the minds of most people, Faith's claims of ScreenMail and InfoBuying made her sound like a raving nut.

But she was right. I saw these things come to pass. You did too.

Solomon's writings in Ecclesiastes and the accuracy of Faith Popcorn's predictions caused me to become sensitive to patterns of events over long periods of time, leading finally to my own November 2003 realization of society's forty-year Pendulum.

When I explained my theory to Dr. Grant, he pointed me to *Generations: The History of America's Future, 1584 to 2069* by William Strauss and Neil Howe.[2] That book gave me the data that showed me I was on solid ground.

Strauss and Howe described four "generations," each of which lasts about twenty years. The pattern is:

1. Idealist, followed by
2. Reactive, followed by
3. Civic, followed by
4. Adaptive, then back to Idealist.

However, I was deeply frustrated as I read *Generations* because I didn't see four generations of twenty years each, as Strauss and Howe did. I saw two generations of forty years each. Finally, a few hundred pages into the book, Strauss and Howe described the Idealist and the Civic generations as *dominant* and the Reactive and Adaptive generations as *recessive*.

That was the moment I began to stitch our two theories together: *the "dominant" twenty-year periods mark the upswing of a pendulum and the "recessive" twenty-year periods mark its downswing, as the values that pushed the pendulum upward begin to run out of steam.*

Society hungers for individuality and freedom during the upswing of a "Me"—nothing wrong with that. But we always take a good thing too far. What begins as a beautiful dream of self-discovery (1963) ends as hollow, phony posing (1983). And then from the heady heights of those glittering disco lights, our desires drift quietly back to earth, feather-like, toward what we left behind: working together for the common good.

Two weeks later, I sent the following "Monday Morning Memo" to fourteen thousand subscribers:

1963 All Over Again

December 15, 2003: We're about to finish 1963 for the second time.

Forty years is how long a true "generation" stays in power, during which time social change will be evolutionary, rather than revolutionary. But in the waning years of each generation, "Alpha Voices" ring out as prophets in the wilderness, providing a glimpse of the new generation that will soon emerge like a baby chick struggling to break out of its shell.

Prior to 1963, Jack Kerouac's *On the Road* and J. D. Salinger's *Catcher in the Rye* were the Alpha Voices that gave us a glimpse of the emerging Baby Boomers. The musical Alphas that rang out five years later (1958) were Chuck Berry and Elvis Presley. Then, at the tipping point—1963—we encountered the Beatles, followed by the Rolling Stones, and the world began rapidly changing stripe and color. The passing of the torch from the duty-bound WWII generation into the hands of the "Do-Your-Own-Thing" Baby Boomers was officially underway.

AOL and Google are the Kerouac and Salinger of the new generation that will soon pry the torch from the hands of boomers reluctant to let it go. Chuck Berry and Elvis Presley have become Tupac Shakur and Eminem, and the Baby Boomers' reaction to them is much like their own parents' reaction to Chuck and Elvis. But instead of saying, "Take a bath, cut your hair, and get a job," we're saying, "Pull those pants up, spin that cap around, and wash your mouth out with soap."

At the peak of the baby boom, there were seventy-four million teenagers in America, and radio carried a generation on its shoulders. Today there are seventy-two million teenagers who are about to take over the world. Do you understand what fuels their passions? Can you see the technological bonds that bind them?

iStockphoto / Photogalia

Baby-boomer heroes were always bigger than life, perfect icons, brash and beautiful: Muhammad Ali, Elvis, James Bond. But the emerging generation holds a different view of what makes a hero.

Boomers rejected conformity, and their attitude swept the land, changing even the mores of their fuddy-duddy parents. But today's teens are rejecting pretense. Born into a world of hype, their internal BS meters are highly sensitive and blisteringly accurate.

iStockphoto / Giorgio Magini

Words like *amazing, astounding,* and *spectacular* are translated as "blah," "blah," and "blah." Consequently, tried-and-true selling methods that worked as recently as a year ago are working far less well today. Trust me, I know. The world is again changing stripe and color. We're at another tipping point. Can you feel it?

No one on earth could read Egyptian hieroglyphics until Napoleon Bonaparte discovered the Rosetta Stone in 1799. That stone—nearly four feet tall—told the same story in three different languages. Two of those languages we could read. The third language was hieroglyphics. Armed with insights gained from studying the Rosetta Stone, the wealth of a whole society, ancient Egypt, became available to those who took the time to learn the strange, new language.

iStockphoto / pearleye

If you are concerned about the changes that you see happening all around you, there are basically two things you can do:

1. Pretend that it won't affect your business. (Let me know how this works out for you.)

2. Search for a Rosetta Stone that will give you a window into the minds of these barbarians at the gate so that in the future at least you'll know how to do business with them.

Bigstock / Zmrlzna

If you choose option number two, I believe you'll find the movie *8 Mile* starring Eminem, playing himself, to be a pretty good place to start.
—*Roy H. Williams*

Should you choose to read Strauss and Howe's *Generations*—and you should—you will notice that our books do not entirely agree. Having come at the same central idea from two different directions, it is reasonable that we should have two different perspectives. And because our book was written twenty years after theirs, Michael and I have had many more years to contemplate, speculate, and investigate this fascinating sociological phenomenon.

With regard to Solomon, Faith Popcorn, William Strauss, and Neil Howe, we can only echo the famous words of Isaac Newton, from a letter written to his friend Robert Hooke on February 5, 1675: *If I have seen further than other men, it is only by standing on the shoulders of giants.*

Thank you, Neil.

Thank you, William.
Thank you, Faith.
Thank you, Solomon.
You are our giants.

Pendulum Legend

"Me" is the gravity of the Moon.

"We" is the momentum of water.

CHAPTER TWO

"We" versus "Me"

The energies of a duality drive the Pendulum of public opinion.
On one side is "Me," the individual—unique, special, and possessing unlimited potential.

Figure 2.1 "ME" cycle.

1. demands freedom of expression;
2. applauds personal liberty;
3. believes one man is wiser than a million men: "A camel is a racehorse designed by a committee";
4. wants to achieve a better life;
5. is about big dreams;
6. desires to be Number One: "I came, I saw, I conquered";
7. admires individual confidence and is attracted to decisive persons;

8. believes leadership is "Look at me. Admire me. Emulate me if you can"; and
9. strengthens a society's sense of identity as it elevates attractive heroes.

On the other side is "We"—the group, the team, the tribe, the collective.

Figure 2.2 "WE" cycle.

1. demands conformity for the common good;
2. applauds personal responsibility;
3. believes a million men are wiser than one man: "Two heads are better than one";
4. wants to create a better world;
5. is about small actions;
6. desires to be a productive member of the team: "I came, I saw, I concurred";
7. admires individual humility and is attracted to thoughtful persons;
8. believes leadership is "This is the problem as I see it. Please consider the things I am telling you and perhaps we can solve this problem together"; and
9. strengthens a society's sense of purpose as it considers all its problems.

"Me" and "We" are the equal-but-opposite attractions that pull society's Pendulum one way, then the other.

The twenty-year Upswing to the Zenith of "We" (e.g., 1923–1943) is followed by a twenty-year Downswing as that "We" cycle loses energy (e.g., 1943–1963). Society then begins a twenty-year Upswing into "Me" (e.g., 1963–1983), followed by a twenty-year Downswing as the "Me" cycle loses energy (1983–2003).

Think of the Pendulum as the forty-year heartbeat of society, systolic and diastolic. Contract and the Pendulum swings upward, relax and the Pendulum swings down again.

Although society gets legalistic and judgmental during a "We," we do accomplish a lot of good things, such as raising the flag over Iwo Jima.

We let our hair down in a "Me" and become quite a mess because of it, but this gives us a particular joy—for example, Jimmy Buffett's "Margaritaville."

"We" and "Me"—it's hard to choose between them.

Figure 2.3 Values and beliefs that motivate society in "WE" and "ME" cycles.

WE	DRIVERS OF A "WE" VS. DRIVERS OF A "ME"	ME

• Demands conformity for the common good.	• Demands freedom of expression.
• Applauds personal responsibility.	• Applauds personal liberty.
• Believes a million men are wiser than one man.	• Believes one man is wiser than a million men.
• Wants to create a better world. "I came, I saw, I *concurred*."	• Wants to achieve a better life: "I came, I saw, I *conquered*."
• Is about small actions.	• Is about big dreams.
• Desires to be part of a productive team.	• Desires to be Number One.
• Admires humility and thoughtful persons.	• Admires individual confidence and decisive persons.
• Believes leadership is "This is the problem as I see it. Let's solve it together."	• Believes leadership is "Look at me. Admire me. Emulate me if you can."
• Strengthen society's sense of purpose, focuses on solving problems.	• Strengthen society's sense of identity, elevates attractive heroes.

Yes, the hardest choices in life are the choices between two good things.

And we always take good things too far.

The beautiful "We" dream of *working together for the common good* gains momentum until it becomes duty, obligation, and sacrifice. What began in joy ends in bondage. This twenty-year Upswing on the "We" side of the Pendulum is what Strauss and Howe called the "civic" generation. The years 1923 to 1943 were just such a twenty-year Upswing.

Suffering the consequences of having taken a good thing too far, society begins to fall away from the extreme. The twenty-year Downswing of the "We" is what Strauss and Howe called the "adaptive" generation (e.g., 1943–1963).

The forty-year Pendulum is now back to its central position, the fulcrum, the tipping point halfway between Zeniths, ready to swing twenty years up to the opposite side as we take another good thing too far.

The beautiful "Me" dream of *individual expression,* "Do your own thing; march to the beat of a different drummer," gains momentum and refinement until it finally becomes plastic, hollow, phony posing. What began in joy now ends in bondage. This twenty-year Upswing of "Me" is what Strauss and Howe called the "idealist" generation. The years 1963–1983 were just such a twenty-year Upswing.

Again suffering the consequences of having taken a good thing too far, society falls back once again from the extreme. The twenty-year Downswing of "Me" is what Strauss and Howe called the "reactive" generation. You and I called it Gen-X (1983–2003).

The Period of 2003–2023 Is Another Upswing of the Pendulum

New York Times columnist David Brooks, writing about students graduating in May of 2011, said,

 Worst of all, they are sent off into this world with the whole baby-boomer theology ringing in their ears. If you sample some of the commencement addresses being broadcast on C-Span

Figure 2.4 Upswing into a "WE" Zenith.

these days, you see that many graduates are told to: Follow your passion, chart your own course, march to the beat of your own drummer, follow your dreams, and find yourself. This is the litany of expressive individualism. But, of course, this mantra misleads on nearly every front.

Brooks further challenged this "Me" idea of finding yourself with a poignant observation:

 Most people don't form a self and then lead a life. They are called by a problem, and the self is constructed gradually by their calling.

Born in 1961, David Brooks is a baby boomer, if you cling to the idea of birth cohorts, but Brooks clearly understands the spirit of "We": *Find a problem and sacrifice yourself to solve it.*

 Finally, graduates are told to be independent-minded and to express their inner spirit. But, of course, doing your job well often means suppressing yourself. As Atul Gawande mentioned during his countercultural address last week at Harvard Medical School, being a good doctor often means being part of a team, following the rules of an institution, going down a regimented checklist.

Written in the ninth year of a "We" Upswing, Brooks ends this insightful column with the words, "The purpose in life is not to find yourself. It's to lose yourself."[1] Society in a "Me" talks about big dreams and possibilities. But society in a "We" says, "Talk is cheap. Don't tell me what you believe. Show me."

Later in this book we'll look at everything the current "We" Upswing has meant so far and make a few predictions about what is likely to happen in the future, but right now let's establish a few definitions.

Upswing of the Pendulum: a window of time, approximately twenty years, when the prevailing set of values is gaining momentum in a society. (The "dominant" generations of Strauss and Howe: Idealist—"Me" and Civic—"We.")

Downswing of the Pendulum: a window of time, approximately twenty years, when the prevailing set of values is losing momentum in a society. (The "recessive" generations of Strauss and Howe: Reactive—"Me" and Adaptive—"We.")

Halfway Up/Halfway Down: the middle of any Upswing or Downswing, that point in time halfway between the fulcrum and the Zenith. The Pendulum is in the same position halfway down as when it is halfway up. Consequently, the outlook of society will be very much the same.

EXAMPLE: The year 1933 was halfway up a "We." In contrast, the year 1953 was halfway down that same "We." The attitudes of those years were very similar. Likewise, 1973 was halfway up a "Me," and 1993 was halfway down that same "Me." Again, the attitudes and music of those years were very similar.

Right now you might be thinking, "Upswing twenty years to the Zenith of 'Me,' then Downswing twenty years to the tipping point, then up twenty years to 'We,' then down twenty years to the tipping point would seem to indicate an eighty-year pattern rather than only forty years." This is true, but transformational change happens during a window of just forty years, between one Zenith of the Pendulum and another. Consequently, a society becomes an entirely different people every forty years.

If this idea of becoming a new people every forty years puts an itch of memory in your brain, it's probably because you're remembering the story of Moses leading Israel through forty years of wandering in the wilderness.

We're Going to Talk About That Later

An ocean wave rolls onto the beach. Are you surprised when it rolls back out again? Neither should you be surprised when history repeats itself. The gravity of the Moon creates the tides. The momentum of water creates the waves.

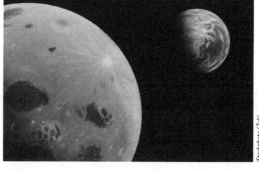

"Me" is the gravity of the Moon. "We" is the momentum of water.

You'll also notice that we don't name the sides of the Pendulum "left" and "right." This is because these words harbor political associations of liberalism and conservatism. Assigning political parties to the sides of the Pendulum is a mistake. One might argue, "But conservatives fight for the rights of the entrepreneur, the individual 'Me,' whereas liberals fight for the benefit of the larger group—trade unions and the environment, the realm of the collective 'We.'" But that's just a single aspect of the conservative-liberal duality. A person might just as easily argue, "Liberals fight for the right of the individual woman, 'Me,' to choose. Conservatives fight for the beliefs of the prevailing religious group, the collective 'We.'"

See how easy it would be to fall into a semantic debate? If you attempt to assign political beliefs to the swings of the Pendulum, you'll become as confused as a termite in a yo-yo. Please resist the temptation.

Likewise, we don't call the sides of the Pendulum "East" and "West" due to the cultural connotations of those words. This too would be a mistake. We've done insufficient research to make this statement conclusively, but it would appear that the Eastern and Western Pendulums are locked in opposite cycles. Western Europe, the Americas, and Australia are headed into a "We" just as China, India, and the rest of Asia seem to be headed into a "Me." In essence, China is experiencing the '60s. Our 1963 happened for them in 2003.

The November 19, 2007, issue of *Newsweek* sports a colorful cover drawn in that style that was unique to the '60s, and in the balloon letters of that era it reads,

1968: The Year That Made Us Who We Are

China in 2008 was flexing its muscles in the glorious springtime that is the Upswing of every "We." Think of the Beijing Olympics of 2008 as the Chinese version of our 1968. As we mentioned earlier, society strengthens its identity in a "Me" as it elevates attractive heroes.

Figure 2.2 *The shift in societal values as "WE" and "ME" cycles approach a Zenith, when we take a good thing too far.*

WHAT HAPPENS WHEN WE TAKE A GOOD THING TOO FAR			
UPSWING WE VALUES	ZENITH WE (TOO FAR) VALUES	UPSWING ME VALUES	ZENITH ME (TOO FAR) VALUES
Responsibility	» Duty	Big dreams	» Hollowness
Humility	» Obligation	Individual expression	» Posing
Thoughtfulness	» Sacrifice	Freedom	» Phoniness
Conformity	» Regimentation	Being cool	» Self-centeredness
Authenticity	» Self-righteousness	Personal achievement	» Guru worship
Transparency	» Oppressiveness	Rose-colored lenses	» Depravity

In 2003, the year of the Western tipping point from the Downswing of "Me" (1983–2003) into the Upswing of our current "We," I sent the following Monday Morning Memo to my few thousand subscribers around the world:

A Society and Its Heroes

Heroes are dangerous things. Bigger than life, highly exaggerated, and always positioned in the most favorable light, a hero is a beautiful lie.

iStockphoto / RUSSELLTATEdotCOM

Did George Washington really chop down a cherry tree and then confess to his father? Could Paul Bunyan really do the work of fifty men in a day? Does billionaire Bruce Wayne really risk his life to help the less fortunate around him?

We have historic heroes, folk heroes, and comic book heroes. We have heroes in books, in songs, in movies, and in sport. We have heroes of morality, leadership, kindness, and excellence. And nothing is so devastating to our sense of well-being as a badly fallen hero. Yes, heroes are dangerous things to have.

The only thing more dangerous is not to have them.

Heroes raise the bar we jump over and hold high the standards we live by. They are ever-present tattoos on our psyche, the embodiment of all we are striving to be.

We create our heroes from our hopes and dreams. And then they attempt to create us in their own image.

It's funny when you think about it: We tell the lie of George Washington and the cherry tree to impress on our children the importance of honesty. We boast of the exploits of Paul Bunyan to communicate the beauty of productivity and the power of a work ethic. And really, wouldn't the world be a better place if all its billionaires were as selfless as Bruce Wayne?

WE But as the romantic and misty-eyed Baby Boomers shuffle off the American stage, they're being replaced by a clear-eyed generation who believes in "keepin' it real," saying always, "Take a good look, dog, 'cause you ain't all that."

New York World-Telegram / Alan Fisher; Mickey Mouse / iStockphoto

So now we put our politicians under a microscope because we won't accept less than the bitter truth. Could JFK have survived the scrutiny we imposed on poor Bill Clinton? The dysfunctional *Malcolm in the Middle* has replaced television's idyllic John-Boy Walton, and a reality show has replaced Sunday night's *Wonderful World of Disney*.

As we reject artificiality and hype, are we also killing off all our heroes?

Two hundred ninety-nine years ago, Andrew Fletcher understood the transforming power of heroes. In his 1704 speech from the floor of the Scottish Parliament, he pleaded for the creation of myths and legends to inspire the Scottish people, saying, "Who should make the laws of a nation? And we find that most of the ancient legislators thought they could not well reform the manners of any city without the help of a lyric, and sometimes of a dramatic poet."

 Yes, every hero is a beautiful lie.
But then so is every dream.
Until it becomes reality.

—Roy H. Williams

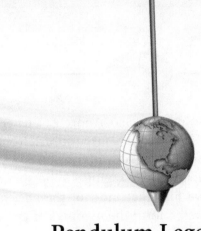

Pendulum Legend

It's not about age; it's about attitude. It's not about when you were born; it's about how you see the world.

CHAPTER THREE

What Defines a Generation?

The classic definition of *generation* in modern conversation is "birth cohorts; people born between a certain year and another certain year."

Using this classic definition of *generation,* a glance online will tell you that baby boomers are considered those people born between 1946 and 1964.

Gen-Xers were born either between 1965 and 1976, between 1965 and 1980, or between 1961 and 1981, depending on who is talking.

Millennials (also called generation y, generation next, net generation, echo boomers, the 9/11 generation, and the Facebook generation) were born between 1977 and 1998, or from 1978 and 2000.

Catherine Colbert, a writer for Bizmology, says, "Millennials in general were born between 1980 and 2005," but then her next words hit the bull's-eye: "The age of this group isn't as important as its attitude."[1]

God bless Colbert. She seems to have realized that anyone who sees the world through the eyes of a millennial and makes judgments and evaluations according to the values of a millennial should rightfully be called a millennial.

iStockphoto / andipantz

It's not about age; it's about attitude. It's not about when you were born; it's about how you see the world.

In this book, the word *generation* will be defined as, "life cohorts bonded by a set of values that dictate the prevailing worldview of the majority."

Life cohorts, not *birth* cohorts. Everyone alive—regardless of their age—who sees the world through the lens of a particular set of values is part of that generation.

Very few people see the world today as they saw it in 1971. Most of the group that was born between 1946 and 1964—typically called baby boomers—have adopted the worldview typically ascribed to millennials. *This means the boomers have lost their boomerness.* A message that would have resonated in their hearts in 1971 will sound corny, contrived, and syrupy today:

ME

I'd like to buy the world a home and furnish it with love, grow apple trees and honeybees and snow-white turtledoves. I'd like to teach the world to sing in perfect harmony. I'd like to buy the world a Coke and keep it company. *It's the real thing: Coca-Cola. What the world wants today: Coca Cola.*

When Coke's famous Hilltop ad appeared on television in 1971, our throats got tight and our eyes got big as we whispered, "It's just so *meaningful.*" But if that original Hilltop ad were played for the first time today, those same boomers would say, "Seriously? Apple trees? Honeybees? Snow-white turtledoves? You're kidding, right? And exactly what has Coca-Cola ever done to facilitate world peace?"

The birth cohorts once called baby boomers see today's world through a different lens than they used forty years ago. They're no longer filtering their perceptions through the same set of values they used in 1972.

People change. We don't remain who we were. This is why advertisers should target not an age group, but a belief system, a worldview, an attitude. (We'll talk more about this and other uses of the Pendulum in Chapter 14.)

New values are introduced every forty years at a *tipping point*, also known as a *fulcrum*. This tipping point/fulcrum is where the Pendulum hangs directly downward, having just completed a Downswing and ready to begin the Upswing on the other side.

On one side of society's Pendulum is "Me," marked by the idealization of individuality and freedom of expression. The values of "Me" are the values of the grasshopper, not the ant. The grasshopper is happy-go-lucky, living always in the moment.

On the other side of the Pendulum is "We," marked by the idealization of authenticity and belonging to a tribe, working together for the common good. The ants are "We," trying to do the right thing, fulfilling their obligations, cleaning up the mess the grasshopper left behind.

A student of psychology may detect in the "Me" and the "We" an echo of Carl Jung's and Edward Edinger's theories regarding the ego and the self. Edinger described this ego/self duality as follows: "The ego is the seat of the subjective identity while the self is the seat of the objective identity."[2] The ego is the "Me," the self, the "We." Dr. Richard D. (Nick) Grant adds, "This creative tension between the 'Me' and the 'We' is the engine of qualitative development throughout life. The answer is neither one nor the other, it's a both/and."

Essentially, the ego is that bundle of wants and needs that looks out at the world from behind a pair of eyeballs. But our relationships with others determine the self. For instance, the ego (Me) may love chocolate, swimming, crossword puzzles, and being noticed and

iStockphoto / Camilo Torres

desired by the opposite sex. But the self (We) of that same woman is determined by her relationship to her children, she is their mother; her husband, she is his partner and wife; her friends, she is their loyal confidante; and her job, she is the manager of a team of agents in a real estate office.

Were this woman to ask herself, "Who am I?" she could answer with any or all of the attributes listed above and be correct. But sometimes these attributes come into conflict, do they not?

The ego, "Me," has personal needs, wants, and cravings, whereas the self, "We," is defined by its relationships and connections.

Think of the ego as a vertical line measuring up and down: "Am I happy?" "Do I have status?" "What do you think of me now that I've said this thing, done this thing, bought this thing?"

The self, "We," is a horizontal line that intersects the vertical. This horizontal line measures near and far. "Am I making a difference?" "Do I matter?" "How close are we now that I've said this thing, done this thing, given this thing away?"

Figure 3.1 *Comparison of the mindset in a "WE" cycle versus that of a "ME" cycle.*

WE	"WE" MINDSET VS. "ME" MINDEST		ME
"UNITED WE STAND, DIVIDED WE FALL"		*"BE #1—SECOND PLACE IS THE FIRST LOSER"*	
VALUES	REJECTS	VALUES	REJECTS
Responsibility	Relationships	Big dreams	Small actions
Humility	Teams	Individual expression	Conformity
Thoughtful	Small actions	Freedom	Self-sacrifice
Conformity	Connecting	Being cool	Self-denial
Authenticity	Volunteerism	Personal achievement	Personal responsibility
Transparency	Common good	Rose-colored lenses	Reality check

This ego-self axis is perhaps most easily understood as the healthy tension that exists between desires and responsibilities. And as Dr. Nick Grant said, "The answer is neither one nor the other, it's a both/and."

According to Edinger, the psychological wellness of an individual (and we believe, by extension, a society) "depends on a living connection with the self (We) via a strong ego-self axis."[3] Sara Emily Perna adds, "Damage to the axis severs the connection between the conscious and unconscious realm, and an array of responses may spring forward from the alienation of the ego [Me] from the self [We]. Violence, hubris, ego inflation, guilt complexes, and self-abuse are common reactions to a split. The first half of life is thusly dedicated to the development of a healthy ego-self axis, the unraveling of the ego from the grasp of the self."

In other words, it's about finding balance. Responsibility, carried too far, becomes slavery. This is the danger of too much "We." Conversely, freedom, carried too far, becomes depravity. This is the danger of too much "Me."

The forces that pull a society two different ways are the ego and the self, the "Me" and the "We. *And we seem to travel between these two attractors as a group.* Both are always present, of course. Even at the Zenith of the Pendulum's arc, the opposing force is there. The position of the Pendulum is merely an indicator of which is currently more fashionable.

However, shifting the perspective of a society doesn't happen with the flip of a switch. There is no single year in which the majority in a society decides to make the jump together. Instead, it's rather like sitting on a riverbank watching canoes float by.

In the lead canoe are those pioneering "Alpha Voices" in literature and technology, the most forward thinkers in a society, fully ten years ahead of the crowd. In the second canoe, five years later, are innovators in music, providing an attitude and a voice to the coming new perspective that the forward thinkers in literature and technology had advanced. Then, five years after that, this new music becomes mainstream, as more and more people begin to embrace the new perspective. This is the "tipping point," when the water begins to move swiftly and the scenery begins changing rapidly. These rapids in the river last six years. At the end of this six-year transitionary window, the pace of change slows dramatically as we begin to take a good thing too far.

Due to the fact that there is no single year when the majority of a society makes the jump to new values together, you'll notice the final year of one perspective is also the beginning year of another. We speak of 1923–1943 as being the Upswing of the "We," and 1943–1963 as the Downswing of the "We." So is 1943 Upswing or Downswing?

It's both. Early adopters of a new perspective begin losing their zeal for the old perspective a little sooner than the majority and late adopters will be found clinging to the old values as much as six years later. Not all the canoes reach the rapids simultaneously.

If a person chooses to get mathematically legalistic about all this and takes the position that a year "must either be one or the other. It can't be part of an Upswing and a Downswing at the same time," then that person will quickly come to the conclusion that each forty-year window of transformation is actually thirty-nine years, not forty. Or they will look at our lists of "We" Zeniths and "Me" Zeniths that happen only once every eighty years and say, "Well, by that same logic, if two windows technically come to seventy-nine years, then a single window must be thirty-nine and a half years."

Okay, you can think of it that way if you want.

But you'll be wrong.

Pendulum Legend

For every action there is an equal and opposite reaction.
—Isaac Newton

CHAPTER FOUR

Duality

Isaac Asimov's famous science fiction series *Foundation* is built on the idea that masses of people are predictable, whereas individuals are not. The protagonist of that series, a mathematician named Hari Seldon, spent his life developing "psychohistory," a branch of sociology analogous to mathematical physics. Leveraging the laws of mass action, psychohistory can predict the future, but only on a large scale; it is unreliable on a small scale.[1]

Like all good science fiction, *Foundation* is built on a central idea that is perfectly plausible.

The ancient Chinese named the recurrent dualities of the universe "yin" and "yang." Modern politicos call them *liberalism* and *conservatism*. Electricians call their dualities *positive* and *negative*. Investors call their dualities *risk* and *reward*. In the movie *Unbreakable*, Samuel L. Jackson speaks of duality theatrically: "Now that we know who you are, I know who I am."

Figure 4.1 *Comparison of the mindset in a "WE" cycle versus that of a "ME" cycle.*

WE	"WE" MINDSET VS. "ME" MINDEST				ME
"UNITED WE STAND, DIVIDED WE FALL"			*"BE #1—SECOND PLACE IS THE FIRST LOSER"*		
VALUES	REJECTS		VALUES	REJECTS	
Responsibility	Relationships		Big dreams	Small actions	
Humility	Teams		Individual expression	Conformity	
Thoughtful	Small actions		Freedom	Self-sacrifice	
Conformity	Connecting		Being cool	Self-denial	
Authenticity	Volunteerism		Personal achievement	Personal responsibility	
Transparency	Common good		Rose-colored lenses	Reality check	

Figure 4.2 *Comparison of Ego vs. Self.*

WE	EGO "WE" VS. SELF "ME"	ME
SEAT OF OBJECTIVE IDENTITY		*SEAT OF SUBJECTIVE IDENTITY*
RESPONSIBILITIES		DESIRES
• Relationships and connections		• Personal wants and needs
• Am I making a difference?		• Am I happy?
• Do I matter?		• Do I have status?
Responsibility carried too far becomes slavery.		**Freedom carried too far becomes depravity.**

But it was Isaac Newton who spoke of duality most famously: "For every action there is an equal, but opposite, reaction."

When faced with the concept of duality, small minds will often cling to one and disparage the other. You know people like this, don't you? You hear them say things like, "It has to be either one way or the other—it can't be both."

When Albert Einstein was serving as the proctor for a university test on advanced theoretical physics, a student raised his hand and said, "Sir, I think there's been a mistake. This is the same test we were given last year." And Albert replied, "Yes, the test is the same as last year, but this year the answers are different."

Albert could just as easily have been talking about society's Pendulum: "This year the answers are different."

> The opposite of a correct statement is a false statement. But the opposite of a profound truth may well be another profound truth.
>
> —***Niels Bohr,*** *physicist, winner of the Nobel Prize for Physics in 1922 for his contributions that were essential to our modern understanding of atomic structure and quantum mechanics, the building blocks of reality.*

As improbable as it sounds, quantum mechanics tells us that matter can be in two places at once. So with your permission, we're going to maintain that the Zenith year of each forty-year cycle can likewise be the final year of an Upswing and the first year of a Downswing simultaneously.

Figure 4.3 Examples of duality.

THE CONCEPT OF DUALITY	
"The opposite of a correct statement is a false statement. But the opposite of a profound truth may well be another profound truth."—Niels Bohr	
• Yin	• Yang
• Positive	• Negative
• Good	• Evil
• Risk	• Reward
• Liberalism	• Conservatism
• Action	• Reaction

Pendulum Legend

When the Pendulum begins a new twenty-year upward climb, the sun shines
more brightly, the birds sing more sweetly, and everyone grows excited as
life itself is reinvented. Magic sparkles in the air.

CHAPTER FIVE

Alpha Voices and the Six-Year Transitionary Window

When the Pendulum has reached a twenty-year Zenith and fallen halfway back to the fulcrum, Alpha Voices emerge in technology and literature, giving us an early glimpse of the new values that will become mainstream in just ten years. These Alpha Voices never realize their own significance at the time; only later do they see that they were the prophets of what was to come.

Everyone in society is aware of these Alpha Voices, though they don't yet know if the Alphas will be a fad or a trend. We discuss them, argue about them, debate their message, and wrestle with their appropriateness. This continues until year thirty-five, when a new, fringe genre of music joins the Alpha Voices, one that gains momentum day by day, accelerating the new values' acceptance that will soon explode into widespread acceptance in the year of the tipping point.

When the tipping point at the fulcrum is finally reached and the Pendulum begins a new twenty-year upward climb, the sun shines more brightly, the birds sing more sweetly, and everyone grows excited as life itself is reinvented. Magic sparkles in the air.

PhotoDune / Solarseven

The new values that the Alpha Voices of technology and literature had hinted at ten years earlier now gain widespread acceptance. This tipping point marks the beginning of that highly predictable, six-year transitionary window in which the majority of society will adopt the new values.

The year 1963 was the tipping point year from a "We" perspective back into the "Me." The people who lived through those years will tell you that 1960 through 1962 weren't really part of the magic called "The '60s"—those years were just the tail end of the '50s.

Look closely and you'll see that all the magic of "the '60s" happened from 1963 to 1968. This was the six-year transitionary window.

Figure 5.1 *Alphas are leaders who herald the changing mindset after a "ME" and "WE" Zenith.*

ROLE OF ALPHAS

THE MAGIC OF THE TRANSITIONARY WINDOWS

WHO:	Authors, artists, and thought leaders
WHAT:	Technology
WHEN:	Literature and technology—ten years after a Zenith
	Music—fifteen years after a Zenith
WHY:	Restore balance

The next tipping point, from "Me" back into "We," occurred in 2003. We'll examine both of these tipping points in detail in later chapters, but right now the only thing that matters is that you understand that 2003 to 2008 was another magical six-year window, although most of us didn't realize it at the time. The further we move away from those years, however, the more we'll recall the magic, the discovery, and the wonder of those sunlit days.

Let's look at those six years. Prior to 2003, the secure transfer of money online was a problem. Uploading a video was an even bigger problem. Search engines were an exercise in frustration.

Figure 5.2 *The Tipping Point from "ME" to "WE."*

iStockphoto / nazdravie

Although Google was incorporated in 1998, those first five years were all about finding focus, struggling with the business model, and wrestling with challengers. In 2003, Google moved into their current location, "The Googleplex" at 1600 Amphitheatre Parkway in Mountain View, California, "to organize the world's information and make it universally accessible and useful."

PayPal™ was purchased by eBay® in October, 2002. In early 2003, PayPal then whooshed into popularity, making e-commerce possible for even the smallest of websites.

Facebook was launched in February, 2004 "to give people the power to share and make the world more open and connected."

Three former PayPal employees created YouTube in February, 2005 "to provide fast and easy video access and the ability to share videos frequently."

Twitter was launched in July, 2006 "to instantly connect people everywhere to what's most important to them."

iStockphoto / Alija

Jimmy Wales launched Wikipedia in 2001. In 2003, it exploded into such a phenomenon that in 2006 *Time* magazine named him one of the world's most influential people.

As we've discussed, birth cohorts don't define a generation; instead, a generation is composed of all the people alive in a society simultaneously—life cohorts.

So do birth cohorts share a common denominator other than an age bracket?

Yes, they most certainly do. Birth cohorts share a specific window of opportunity upon their coming-of-age. Malcolm Gladwell makes this point quite powerfully in his book *Outliers: The Story of Success* showing the names and fortunes of the seventy-five wealthiest people in the history of the world calculated in current US dollars. An astounding fourteen of these seventy-five billionaires were Americans born in a nine-year window centered in 1835.

iStockphoto / Daft_Lion_Studio

This was when the railroads were being built and when Wall Street emerged. It was when industrial manufacturing started in earnest. It was when all the rules by which the traditional economy had functioned were broken and remade. . . . If you were born in the late 1840s you missed it. You were too young to take advantage of that moment. If you were born in the 1820s, you were too old: your mind-set was shaped by the pre–Civil War paradigm. But there was a particular, narrow nine-year window that was just perfect for seeing the potential that the future held.[1]

Thus, your birth year does not determine your attitudes and beliefs, but it does determine your opportunities. History has proven this again and again.

Pendulum Legend

The Pendulum predicts only the momentum and direction of the majority in a society; most of the people, most of the time. Certainly not everyone. Certainly not always.

CHAPTER SIX

The Limits of Predictability

There are two reasons you'll have no trouble finding exceptions to what is presented in this book:

1. There is always a counterculture within a prevailing culture.
2. Individuals are not predictable.

The Pendulum predicts only the momentum and direction of the *majority* in a society—most of the people, most of the time.

Certainly not everyone, and certainly not always.

We mention this not because we fear detractors, but rather because there are zealots who will try to use these insights to make predictions that, frankly, cannot be made.

We must keep in mind the story of the statistician who drowned while trying to wade across a river with an average depth of four feet. That is to say, in a culture that reveres statistics, we can never be sure what sort of nonsense will lodge in people's heads.[1]

WE

In the darkness of "We" you'll find smug self-righteousness, legalism and bureaucracy.

—*Michael R. Drew*

Here's a theoretical example of the dangerous "zealot logic" we're talking about:

Al Gore, a Democrat, won the popular vote in the election of 2000, but the presidency went to George W. Bush, the son of a president, amidst outraged cries of "bargain and corruption." This had already happened once before when Andrew Jackson, another Democrat, won the popular vote in 1824 but the presidency went to John Quincy Adams, the son of a president, amidst outraged cries of "bargain and corruption." The only difference between the two scenarios is that Andrew Jackson ran again four years later and soundly defeated John Quincy Adams to become our seventh president. The Pendulum, therefore, predicts that if Al Gore had run again in 2004, he most certainly would have been elected.

When you think about it for a moment, it does seem likely that Gore would have been elected had he run a second time in 2004. But this does *not* prove the absurd claim that it was predictable using Pendulum theory. As we told you earlier, we strongly discourage any use of the Pendulum to make specific predictions concerning politics or the economy.

Sparkling goodness with a dark underbelly attends each of the twenty-year strokes of the Pendulum. None of them is inherently better than the others. The only time when things will, more often than not, be upbeat is when the Pendulum is near its fulcrum halfway between extremes. This is when the tension between "Me" and "We" is most in balance and a society hums in expectant harmony.

Transparency, volunteerism, and authenticity are on the sunny side of a "We." But in the darkness of "We" you'll find smug self-righteousness, legalism, and bureaucracy.

The year 2003 was the beginning of a "We," and we're currently in its Upswing. To better understand what lies ahead, let's look back at the previous Upswing of "We."

Come, the journey continues.

Pendulum Legend

Togetherness, connection, working together for the common good—these are the dreams that unite us in every Upswing of a "We."

CHAPTER SEVEN

1923–1933:
First Half of the
Upswing into "We"

It is notable that Aesop's Film Fables produced the first version of *The Ants and the Grasshopper* (1921) just prior to the tipping point of 1923. Then, just one year past the Zenith of the "We," Walt Disney produced his own version, *The Grasshopper and the Ants* (1934), and then visited the fable once again in *Mickey and the Big Storm,* in which Donald Duck and Goofy spend the first day of a winter snowstorm playing in the snow and don't bother to stock up on supplies. Fortunately for them, the story's "We" hero, Mickey, has packed more than enough for himself and all his friends.

The grasshopper's lack of responsibility is underlined by the song, "The World Owes Me a Living," sung by superstar Shirley Temple in the 1934 film *Now and Forever.*

Oh, I owe the world a living....
You ants were right the time you said
"You've got to work for all you get."

Keep in mind that the fable of "The Grasshopper and the Ant" has been around for more than twenty-five hundred years. Along with "The Fox and the Grapes," "The Tortoise and the Hare," and "The Boy

Who Cried Wolf," it's one of the fables of Aesop, a storytelling slave who lived in ancient Greece between 620 and 560 BCE.

This particular story involves a grasshopper that spends the warm months singing and playing while the ants work diligently to store up food for winter. When those icy winds arrive and the ground is covered with snow, the grasshopper finds itself dying of hunger and asks the ants for food, only to be rebuked for his idleness. The grasshopper then dies miserably while the ants enjoy the winter, snug and warm and with bellies full. *The End.*

At least that's how we spin the story during the Upswing of a "We."

Figure 7.1 Moving toward the Zenith of "WE."

In 1564, just one year past the tipping point into the Upswing of a "Me," Gabriele Faerno published a poem in Latin that tells of an ant that was once a man who was always busy farming. Sounds familiar, right? But this man, tirelessly working and obsessed with gathering, also plundered his neighbors' crops at night. This angered the king of the gods, who turned him into an ant. But even as an ant, the man still roamed the fields, gathering and storing food for the future.

MESSAGE: Ants are tedious workaholics.

Roger L'Estrange published a similar pro-grasshopper spin more than a century later, saying the ant's "Vertue and Vice, in many Cases, are hardly Distinguishable but by the Name."

In 1922, a literary indictment was published that spoke of America's loss of personal, moral, and spiritual values. The 434 lines of this indictment energized and unified the nation as we marched dutifully into a "We." The indictment was T. S. Eliot's *The Waste Land*, one of the most important poems of the twentieth century.

WE What are the roots that clutch, what branches grow
Out of this stony rubbish? Son of man,
You cannot say, or guess, for you know only
A heap of broken images . . .
And I will show you something different from either
Your shadow at morning striding behind you
Or your shadow at evening rising to meet you;
I will show you fear in a handful of dust.

Eliot seemed to have been saying that our dreams were "only a heap of broken images" and that we were aware mostly of our own shadows—that moment-by-moment existence we call life. But "I will show you fear in a handful of dust." Eliot spoke of the consequences of our actions and the certainty of our mortality: ashes to ashes, dust to dust.

F. Scott Fitzgerald's *The Great Gatsby* was published in 1925, during the third year of the six-year transitionary window. It moved the reader neatly from the "Me" American dream that anyone can achieve anything to the rapidly growing "We" perspective that individual achievement is ultimately empty.

The book introduces Tom and Daisy Buchanan as part of the "old aristocracy." Tom was a football player in college and is now a wealthy dilettante who plays polo and has a mistress. His wife, Daisy, is attractive, pampered, and superficial, largely ignoring her three-year-old daughter. Jay Gatsby is a millionaire bootlegger who is wrongly murdered while floating in his pool. Although hundreds of socialites had attended Gatsby's lavish parties, almost no one attends his funeral. In the end, the wealthy "Me" people in *The Great Gatsby* suffer due to their questionable morals. Nick, the narrator, disgusted with them, returns to his home in the Midwest.

Another huge book published during this six-year transitionary window was Ernest Hemingway's *The Sun Also Rises* in 1926. A summary of this book in Wikipedia includes the following paragraph:

 Hemingway admired hard work. He portrayed the matadors and the prostitutes, who work for a living, in a positive manner, but Brett, who prostitutes herself, is emblematic of "the rotten crowd" living on inherited money. It is Jake, the working journalist, who pays the bills again and again when those that can pay do not. Hemingway shows, through Jake's actions, his disapproval of people who did not pay up. [Hemingway's biographer] Reynolds says that Hemingway shows the tragedy, not so much of the decadence of the Montparnasse crowd, but of *the self-destruction of American values of the period.* As such the author created an American hero who is impotent and powerless. Jake becomes the moral center of the story. He never considers himself part of the expatriate crowd because he is a working man; to Jake a working man is genuine and authentic, and those who do not work for a living spend their lives posing.[1]

Keep in mind that *The Sun Also Rises* was written during the transitionary window from a "Me" about big dreams and personal achievement to a "We" about small actions and personal responsibility.

Published in the seventh year of the Upswing, William Faulkner's *The Sound and the Fury* details the moral decay of the Old South. It is instructive that Faulkner took his title from a famous line in Shakespeare's *Macbeth:*

 Life's but a walking shadow, a poor player
That struts and frets his hour upon the stage
And then is heard no more: it is a tale
Told by an idiot, full of sound and fury,
Signifying nothing.

The emptiness of individuality is an overarching theme of *The Sound and the Fury.*

Fitzgerald, Hemingway, and Faulkner were the literary giants during the Upswing of the last "We," and the values they communicated were identical.

Dr. Albert Schweitzer spent the Upswing of the "We" working among the poor in Africa. He wrote extensively about his experiences and motivations. His opinions and concepts became acknowledged not only in Europe but also worldwide. He said,

 I don't know what your destiny will be, but one thing I know: the only ones among you who will be really happy are those who have sought and found how to serve. [2]

This "We" period also marked the spread of ready-to-wear fashion. Women were joining the job market and didn't want to spend time sewing or being fitted for tailor-made clothes. As class distinctions were blurring, the status symbol aspect of fashion was losing its importance.

But what about the hit songs of that six-year transitionary window?

WE Popular music is a mirror that shows us collectively who we are.

—*Michael R. Drew*

All the big songs spoke of "togetherness" or expressed the pain of a lack of it. One of the marks of a "We" is that although we try to do the right thing, *we whine about it.* The song lyrics of a "Me" celebrate the moment and look forward. The lyrics of a "We" bemoan the moment and look back. Throughout the rest of the book, we'll look at what the majority of Western society was singing as the Pendulum swung from "We" to "Me" and back again. The song lyrics have been abbreviated to only one or two lines that capture the mood and message of the song.

Do you remember the Disney movie *Winnie the Pooh?* Eeyore the donkey is the perfect spokesperson for a "We." His general response is to sigh deeply and moan, "Somebody's got to do it, and it's probably me. Oh, well. Let's get started."

The top songs of the era reflect this sentiment:

Figure 7.2   Popular music themes during the first half of an upswing into "WE."

WE POPULAR MUSIC THEMES: FIRST HALF OF AN UPSWING INTO "WE" (1923–1933)

A TIME OF DUTY, OBLIGATION, AND SACRIFICE

1923: "Downhearted Blues," Bessie Smith

	MESSAGE
Trouble, trouble, I've had it all my days It seems that trouble's going to follow me to my grave.	Life is not a bed of roses. 

1924: "It Had To Be You," Isham Jones

Why do I do just as you say? Why must I just give you your way?	You're bossy and mean, but I love you anyway.

1925: "The Prisoner's Song," Vernon Dalhart

I'll be carried to the new jail tomorrow Leaving my poor darling all alone.	I'm lonely and I wish I wasn't lonely, but I'm going to remain lonely.

1926: "Bye Bye Blackbird," Gene Austin

No one here can love and understand me Oh, what hard luck stories they all hand me.	Life has been dark up until now, but I'm going to make a change.

1927: "My Blue Heaven," Gene Austin

When whippoorwills call And evening is nigh I hurry to my Blue Heaven.	It's getting dark out there, but I've got all I need.

1928: "T for Texas," Jimmie Rodgers

T for Texas, T for Tennessee T for Thelma The gal that made a wreck out of me.	Love hurts, and I'm angry about it.

Popular music is a mirror that shows us collectively who we are. There is no better way to gauge the values and perceptions of a society than to examine its popular music.

These weary and sad song lyrics might make sense if they were written during the Great Depression, but these were the hit songs during the so-called Roaring Twenties, when the United States was in the midst of a boom economy. The stock market didn't crash until 1929, so, please, let's not hear any nonsense about how popular literature and music are tied to economic cycles. The evidence clearly denies this.

Other Expressions of "Coming Together"

In its purest form, the central idea of communism is "working together for the common good." So it should come as no surprise that 1922, the first year of an Upswing into "We," was the year in which the Union of Soviet Socialist Republics (USSR) was established in Europe. It should also not surprise you that this Union fell apart at the Zenith of the "Me," but we're getting ahead of ourselves.

In the United States, we came together in a different way. Radio in 1923 was the Internet of that day, a cheap and convenient way of communicating ideas and information to "the group." Early radio broadcasts were primarily news and world affairs. Later in that decade, radios were used to communicate fears about communism, "The Red Menace."

Although radio had been invented earlier, it took the beginning of a "We" to trigger radio's sweep across the United States. The first broadcasting station created for the general public, KDKA, was launched in Pittsburgh in the early 1920s, just before the tipping point into the Upswing of the "We." Entire families would sit around the radio in Pittsburgh and listen to whatever was broadcast.

In just six short years, new radio stations popped up by the thousands, and listening to the radio had become a national obsession, much like texting, Twitter, and Facebook would become at the

beginning of the next "We." Our hunger in a "We" is to *connect*.

Radio impacted the United States exactly like the Internet would impact it eighty years later: exposing the nation to new ideas and new entertainment, as well as causing us to form opinions on matters to which we had not been previously exposed.

According to Elizabeth Stevenson in *Babbits and Bohemians: From the Great War to the Great Depression*:

 Radio strengthened a tendency already working to make the people of the United States feel united and whole; for the first time, it seemed as if they could have thoughts and feelings simultaneously. For certain individuals, this was comforting and strengthening. It had the effect of making people wish to have simultaneous sensations.[3]

She went on to state that, "The new hobby of radio listening encouraged the tendency . . . a feeling that one's country and oneself were exempt from unpleasant consequences."[4]

 The false advertising of radio advertisements helped to create a sense of ignorance among most Americans towards anything unpleasant. Even though radio had brought the nation together as a whole, it also had the unfortunate side effect of making people of the 1920s more close-minded, ignorant, and disillusioned. Perhaps it was the sense of denial and false hope created by radio that made America so mentally unprepared for the Great Stock Market Crash and the Great Depression.

In a "We,"

1. there will be a widespread hunger to come together;
2. technologies that facilitate this "coming together" will flourish; and

3. society will begin to think itself invincible—the illusion of "United We Stand, Divided We Fall" *is that we cannot fall if we are united.*

This expression "United we stand, divided we fall" can be traced back to "The Four Oxen and the Lion," another fable of Aesop, but its embrace as a defining statement of America can be traced to "The Liberty Song," a Revolutionary War song of John Dickinson published in the *Boston Gazette* in July 1768—*five years into the Upswing of a "We,"* during the magical six-year transitionary window. Notice how the song encourages coming together for the common good: "Then join hand in hand, brave Americans all! By uniting we stand, by dividing we fall!"

But let's jump back to Aesop for a moment, that man who extolled the virtues of the ant in "The Grasshopper and the Ant" and gave us the phrase "United we stand, divided we fall" in his "The Four Oxen and the Lion." For these fables to have gained sufficient traction to be remembered for twenty-five hundred years, Aesop would almost certainly have to have been an Alpha Voice at the thirty-year point of a "Me"—in the middle of a Downswing toward a "We."

Figure 7.3 Values of society during a "WE" cycle.

WE	MINDSET	
"UNITED WE STAND, DIVIDED WE FALL"		
• Responsibility	• Relationships	
• Humility	• Teams	
• Thoughtful	• Small actions	
• Conformity	• Connecting	
• Authenticity	• Volunteerism	
• Transparency	• Common good	

iStockphoto / whitemay

Aesop was born in 620 BCE and died in 560 BCE. We can assume that he wrote his fables during the second half of his life. Do the math and you'll see that the year of his birth, 620 BCE, was just three years before the Zenith of a "We" (617 BCE). This means that Aesop grew up during the Downswing of a "We," was forty-three at the Zenith of a "Me" (577 BCE), and died at the age of sixty, just three years before the tipping point into the Upswing of another "We." This means Aesop would have been fifty-three years old at the time of the Alpha Voices. His canon of fables would have been nearly complete at that time, precisely ten years before those "We" values exploded into the mainstream of Greek society.

Alpha Voices often become immortalized.

Another "connecting us together" invention that swept America during the "We" Upswing of 1923 through 1928 was the automobile.

The prosperity of these years was owed in part to the public funds the US government poured into the economy for the construction of roads and highways. Cars were connecting people everywhere. According to Kenneth Bruce, author of *YOWSAH! YOWSAH! YOWSAH! The Roaring Twenties,*

 [T]here were very few good roads outside the east coast; crossing the continent was a real adventure, as during the spring when the snow melted or after a good rain storm, automobiles would sink into gumbo mud up to their hubs. Travelers crossing Iowa or Nebraska were often forced to wait several days until the road dried before moving on to the next town.[5]

In 1921, the Federal Aid Highway Act offered federal money to state legislatures to stimulate them to organize highway departments. Spurred by these federal dollars, the states launched ambitious road-building programs. Soon, highway construction employed more men than any other industry.

Figure 7.4 Drivers of a "WE" cycle.

WE	DRIVERS OF A "WE" CYCLE
1. Conforms for the common good.	**6.** Desires to be part of a productive team.
2. Assumes personal responsibility.	**7.** Values humility and thoughtful persons.
3. Believes a million men are wiser than one man.	**8.** Believes leadership is "This is the problem as I see it. Let's solve it together."
4. Wants to create a better world: "I came, I saw, I concurred."	**9.** Focuses on solving problems to strengthen society's sense of purpose.
5. Small actions.	

Roads were built to connect us on the ground, just as radios connected us through the airwaves.

The car craze touched every corner of the American economy—stimulating the oil industry, boosting road construction, and creating a housing boom in suburbs.

Henry Ford was the Bill Gates of his generation. In 1923, he earned $264,000 a day, and the Associated Press declared him a billionaire. He paid a record $2,467,946 in taxes for the year 1924.

Factories that had produced armaments for World War I were refitted to produce household appliances. "The primary reason why Americans bought so many household appliances was to simplify everyday tasks such as dishwashing or cutting grass, so that they could spend more time with their families."[6]

Togetherness, connection, working together for the common good—these are the dreams that unite us in every Upswing of a "We," and they are good things, indeed.

But we always take good things too far.

The installment plan, buying on credit, was another product of the 1920s. Money flowed like water. In the spring of 1929, the New York Stock Exchange was more active than it had ever been. Experts predicted "a permanent high plateau." The glorious six-year transitionary window into that "We" was 1923 through 1928.

And you already know what happened on October 24, 1929: the stock market crashed, and our belief in "We" was put to the test.

Sadly, America had just elected Herbert Hoover. Born August 10, 1874, Hoover was eight years old when the Upswing began a forty-year "Me." Consequently, he learned politics during a "Me," and being a politician, he was unable to swing into "We" as quickly as the general public. Hoover was tragically out of step. Even worse, his previous job had been Secretary of Commerce for the previous two administrations, those of Warren G. Harding and Calvin Coolidge. In effect, he had been on the steering committee that landed our ship on the rocks.

As the Depression deepened, Hoover launched public projects to create jobs, but he steadfastly resisted feeding the poor. But this rigid adherence to conservative principles was not his greatest problem. Trained as a mining engineer at Stanford, Hoover came across as mean-spirited and uncaring. Consequently, the shantytowns of the homeless were called "Hoovervilles."

To make matters worse, Hoover supported and signed into law a tariff act in 1930 that triggered international trade wars and made the Depression even worse. Like George W. Bush in his second term, Hoover was a "Me" president in the early years of a "We."

His opposition in the election of 1928 was Alfred Smith, a Democrat, the first Roman Catholic ever to be nominated to run for president. Protestant Americans were afraid to elect a Catholic president, particularly during the Upswing of a "We," when working as a group was the ultimate ideal, because the American public believed the election of a Catholic would put one man, the Pope, in charge of our nation. As a result, Hoover won 58 percent of the popular vote and 444 of 531 electoral votes.

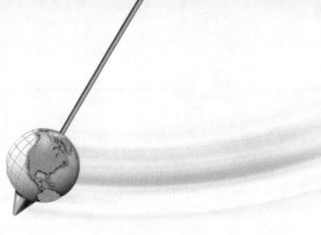

Pendulum Legend

The first six years of any Upswing are beautiful, but then
things begin to smell funny as we get our first good whiff of
"taking a good thing too far."

CHAPTER EIGHT

1933–1943:
The Second Half of the Upswing, Reaching the Zenith of "We"

Make no mistake about it: we'll find something to unite us during a "We."

Take, for instance, 1933, when we were halfway to the Zenith. The motto of that year seemed to be: "Let's keep working together for the common good."

Technological advances included the introduction of intercontinental flights on commercial airplanes, scotch tape, and frozen foods. But halfway up isn't when we hear Alpha Voices in technology and literature giving us a clue of the new perspective that will soon arrive; those Alpha Voices don't emerge until the Pendulum is halfway down.

The first six years of any Upswing are beautiful, but then things begin to smell funny as we get our first good whiff of "taking a good thing too far."

Figure 8.1 *The second half of an upswing of a "WE" cycle.*

The halfway point of an Upswing of "We" isn't a time of heroes but of antiheroes. In the mid-thirties in America, it was: "Let's track down Pretty Boy Floyd, and John Dillinger, and Bonnie and Clyde, and Al Capone. Let's clean this place up and make everyone start acting right."

These impulses are the same in every society, but different countries have different ideas about *what* needs to be cleaned up and *who* isn't acting right.

 The focus of every 'We' is to identify problems, catalog them, assign blame, and elevate regret. 'We' tends to look over its shoulder at the past.

—Michael R. Drew

The year 1933 in Germany was when the book burnings began. Friedrich Schönemann of the University of Berlin spoke at the Chicago Council on Foreign Relations in the autumn of that year. When someone from the floor questioned him about Germany's books burnings, Schönemann replied, "A tremendous flood of books on nudism and of a general pornographic nature unfit for either juvenile or adult reading had inundated Germany, and these were burned. I am sorry to say," he continued, "that the authors of many—of a majority—were Jewish."

According to Kathleen McLaughlin, writing for the *New York Times* in 1933, "These cheap dismissals were met with more yelling from the crowd, including shouts about the fate of the books of writers such as Helen Keller and Albert Einstein. Schönemann showed he would be swayed neither by emotion nor facts: 'No foreign books were burned. I think I am correct in saying that none of Miss Keller's volumes was included.'"[1]

Figure 8.2   Characteristics of society at the Zenith of a "WE" cycle.

WE	ZENITH CHARACTERISTICS

TAKING A GOOD THING TOO FAR

"WHEN A STUPID MAN IS DOING SOMETHING HE IS ASHAMED OF, HE ALWAYS DECLARES THAT IT IS HIS DUTY."—George Bernard Shaw

- Personal liberties stripped away
- Self-righteous
- Duty, obligation, sacrifice
- Secretly dissatisfied

- Long for freedom
- Regimentation
- Process smothers innovation
- Claustrophobic and oppressive

Meanwhile, Franklin Delano Roosevelt called the nation together with the first of his famous Fireside Chats heard on radios nationwide. Roosevelt said, in effect, *Gather around, children. We'll pull through this. We'll all work together for the common good. Gather 'round the radio, children! It's time for a fireside chat!*

Here are some excerpts from that first Fireside Chat, broadcast from the White House on March 12, 1933. Notice how FDR speaks to the nation as if to a family of equals and appeals to everyone to work together for the common good. Notice also the absence of bluster and the overall tone of transparency. These are the stylistic hallmarks of an Upswing of "We."

WE I want to talk for a few minutes with the people of the United States about banking . . . I want to tell you what has been done in the last few days and why it was done, and what the next steps are going to be. . . . I owe this in particular because of the fortitude and good temper with which everybody has accepted the inconvenience and hardships of the banking holiday. I know that when you understand what we in Washington have been about, I shall continue to have your cooperation as fully as I have had your sympathy and help during the past week.

First of all let me state the simple fact that when you deposit money in a bank the bank does not put the money into a safe deposit vault. It invests your money in many different forms of credit—in bonds, in commercial paper, in mortgages, and in many other kinds of loans. In other words, the bank puts your money to work to keep the wheels of industry and of agriculture turning around. A comparatively small part of the money you put into the bank is kept in currency—an amount which in normal times is wholly sufficient to cover the cash needs of the average citizen. In other words the total amount of all the currency in the country is only a comparatively small proportion of the total deposits in all the banks of the country.

What, then, happened during the last few days of February and the first few days of March? Because of undermined confidence on the part of the public, there was a general rush by a large portion of our population to turn bank deposits into currency or gold—a rush so great that the soundest banks could not get enough currency to meet the demand. The reason for this was that on the spur of the moment it was, of course, impossible to sell perfectly sound assets of a bank and convert them into cash except at panic prices far below their real value.

By the afternoon of March 3, scarcely a bank in the country was open to do business. Proclamations closing them, in whole or in part, had been issued by the governors in almost all the states.

It was then that I issued the proclamation providing for the national bank holiday, and this was the first step in the government's reconstruction of our financial and economic fabric.

Let me make it clear to you that the banks will take care of all needs . . . and it is my belief that hoarding during the past week has become an exceedingly unfashionable pastime. . . . I can assure you, my friends, that it is safer to keep your money in a reopened bank than it is to keep it under the mattress.

The success of our whole national program depends, of course, upon the cooperation of the public—on its intelligent support and use of a reliable system.

One more point before I close. There will be, of course, some banks unable to reopen without being reorganized. The new law allows the government to assist in making these reorganizations quickly and effectively and even allows the government to subscribe to at least a part of any new capital that may be required.

I hope you can see, my friends, from this essential recital of what your government is doing that there is nothing complex, nothing radical in the process.

We have had a bad banking situation. Some of our bankers had shown themselves either incompetent or dishonest in their handling of the people's funds. They had used the money entrusted to them in speculations and unwise loans. This was of course not true in the vast majority of our banks, but it was true in enough of them to shock the people of the United States, for a time, into a sense of insecurity and to put them into a frame of mind where they did not differentiate, but seemed to assume that the acts of a comparative few had tainted them all. And so it became the government's job to straighten out this situation and do it as quickly as possible. And the job is being performed. . . .

I can never be sufficiently grateful to the people for the loyal support they have given me in their acceptance of the judgment that has dictated our course, even though all of our processes may not have seemed clear to them.

After all there is an element in the readjustment of our financial system more important than currency, more important than gold, and that is the confidence of the people themselves. Confidence and courage are the essentials of success in carrying out our plan. You people must have faith;

you must not be stampeded by rumors or guesses. Let us unite in banishing fear. We have provided the machinery to restore our financial system, and it is up to you to support and make it work.

It is your problem, my friends, your problem no less than it is mine. *Together we cannot fail.*²

When I presented the first ninety-minute "Pendulum" presentation in Stockholm in January, 2004, I embedded into my Power-Point presentation the first two sentences of that historic fireside chat in FDR's own voice. As the glistening voice of FDR faded, I smiled and said, "Let's hope the American economy doesn't repeat in 2009 what it did in 1929." I distinctly remember that no one laughed, not even a chuckle. Evidently those Europeans held a premonition of the financial implosion that would occur due to the mortgage meltdown crisis of late 2008, just one year prior to the eightieth anniversary of the stock market crash of 1929, when society's Pendulum was in the same position and headed in the same direction as it was in 1929.

When Lehman Brothers and other important financial institutions failed in September, 2008, $150 billion were withdrawn from US money funds in a two-day period. This was thirty times higher than the average two-day outflow. In effect, the money market was subject to a bank run.

Was this collapse avoidable? Absolutely. *The reason history must repeat itself is because we pay too little attention the first time.*

Just to make sure that the values and perspective of the public are continuing in the same direction as they did in 1923, let's look at the top five best-selling novels of 1933:

iStockphoto / magnetcreative

Figure 8.3   Popular novel themes moving toward the Zenith of a "WE" cycle.

WE   POPULAR NOVEL THEMES: REACHING ZENITH OF "WE" (1933–1943)

A TIME OF DUTY, OBLIGATION, AND SACRIFICE	MESSAGE

"Anthony Adverse"
Hervey Allen

Duty and obligation

An orphan's debt to the man who raised him threatens to separate him forever from the woman he loves.

"As the Earth Turns"
Gladys Hasty Carroll

Disillusionment and loss
of innocence

A year in the life of a rural family facing the modern world of airplanes, college educations, and city life.

"Ann Vickers"
Sinclair Lewis

Personal suffering while
helping others

Social worker/prison reformer looks for love with men who abuse her.

"Magnificent Obsession"
Lloyd C. Douglas

Duty and obligation, personal
sacrifice for the benefit of others

A rescue crew resuscitates a man after a boating accident. Consequently, the crew is unable to save the life of a doctor, renowned for his ability to help people, who was having a heart attack on the other side of the lake at the same time. The man who was saved decides to devote his life to making up for the loss of the doctor's life.

iStockphoto / Icodacci

"One More River"
John Galsworthy

The injustice in life, the pain
of love

A young woman flees to England to escape her sadistic husband, falls in love, and becomes hopelessly compromised with a penniless young Englishman.

Nope. No big surprises there. All of these novels are about people trying to do the right thing and suffering for their decisions.

Hit Songs of the Era

Let's look at the final six years leading up to the Zenith of the "We," as the once-beautiful dream of "working together for the common good" becomes duty, obligation, and sacrifice. Although we try to do the right thing during a "We," we also whine and moan about it. Notice how the number-one song each year reminisces wistfully about happier days:

Figure 8.4   Popular song themes moving toward the Zenith of a "WE" cycle.

WE POPULAR SONG THEMES: REACHING ZENITH OF "WE" (1933–1943)	
A TIME OF DUTY, OBLIGATION, AND SACRIFICE	
1938: "Begin the Beguine," Artie Shaw	MESSAGE
And now when I hear people curse the chance that was wasted, I know but too well what they mean.	**Yesterday was better than today.**
1939: "Over the Rainbow," Judy Garland	
And wake up where the clouds are far behind me, Where troubles melt like lemon drops . . .	**Other places are better than this place.**
1940: "In the Mood," Glenn Miller	
Who's the lovin' daddy with the beautiful eyes What a pair o' lips, I'd like to try 'em for size.	**I have needs that aren't currently being met.**
1941: "Chattanooga Choo Choo," Glenn Miller	
Chattanooga choo choo, Won't you choo choo me home?	**I'm gettin' outa here and goin' to a better place.**
1942: "White Christmas," Bing Crosby	
I'm dreaming of a white Christmas Just like the ones I used to know.	**I'm thinking back about good times of the past.**

| I'd rather have a paper doll to call my own | **Someone did me wrong.** |
| Than have a fickle-minded real live girl. | |

The Zenith of a "We" is when "working together for the common good" becomes

- duty ("Be loyal to your union brothers. Don't be a scab."),
- obligation ("You have to be a union member to work here."), and
- sacrifice ("Yes, union dues are high. But we've got to stick together.").

The power of organized labor in the United States peaked in the early 1940s, wielding unbelievable power and influence. In 1941, 10.5 million workers belonged to a labor union; by 1945 that number had reached 14.7 million.

Likewise, the armed forces enjoyed a surge in enlistments prior to the Zenith of the "We" in 1943. By the summer of 1942, men disappeared in vast numbers from the workplace. More than six million women took wartime jobs in factories or filled in for men working on farms, three million volunteered with the Red Cross, and more than two hundred thousand women served in the military.

"We" is looking for problems to fix. Consequently, the focus of every "We" is to identify problems, catalog them, assign blame, and elevate regret. "We" tends to look over its shoulder at the past.

It would be easy to say, "Well, that behavior was just due to the war effort." So why do we always feel more justified in a war effort during a "We?" The wars of which America is most proud—the Revolutionary War and World War II—both occurred during the Upswing of a "We." The wars we barely stumbled through all happened during a "Me."

Does a war cause the "We" or does a "We" cause the war?

A "We" is merely a hunger to come together and work for the common good. It has no agenda of its own. A "We" can easily be aimed at any problem a society chooses.

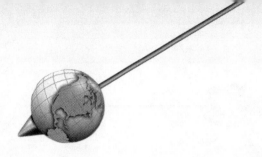

Pendulum Legend

People will usually do in reality what they have seen themselves do
in their minds. Heroes make us see grand possibilities—
first we see it, then we do it.
—*Michael R. Drew*

CHAPTER NINE

Three Thousand Years of "We" and the Origin of Western Society

The saying, "The sun never sets on the British Empire" was true as recently as 1937, when tiny England did, in fact, still have colonies in each of the world's twenty-four time zones. The British explored, conquered, and ruled much of the world for many years. *But what made them believe they could do it?*

For the first thousand years after Christ, Greece and Rome were the only nations that told stories of heroes and champions. England was just a dreary little island of rejects, cast-offs, barbarians, and losers. So who inspired tiny, foggy England to rise up and take over the world?

Hoping to give his countrymen a set of values and a sense of pride, a simple Welsh monk named Geoffrey assembled a complete history of Britain that gave his people a grand and glorious pedigree. Written in 1136, Geoffrey's *History of the Kings of Britain* was a detailed account of the deeds of the British people for each of the seventeen centuries prior to 689 CE.

But not a single word of it was true.

Yet in creating Merlyn, Guinevere, Arthur, and the Knights of the Round Table from the fabric of his imagination, Geoffrey of Monmouth convinced a sad, little island of rejects, cast-offs, barbarians, and losers to see themselves as a magnificent nation.

When they began seeing themselves differently, they soon became a different nation in reality.

It has always been assumed that legends and myths, with their stories of heroes, are the by-products of great civilizations. *But I believe they are the cause of them.* Throughout history, the mightiest civilizations have been the ones with heroes—those larger-than-life role models who inspire ordinary citizens to rise up and do amazing things.

People will usually do in reality what they have seen themselves do in their minds. Heroes make us see grand possibilities—first we see it, then we do it.

The ideas that form the basis of Western society have their roots in ancient Israel and Persia, then Greece, whose culture dominated when Alexander the Great conquered virtually all the known world. However, because Alexander died young and left no strong government behind, the Romans picked up the pieces to form an empire that would provide us with a framework for society until the British Empire emerged.

The primary influencers have been:

- Israel and Persia in the Near East
- Ancient Greece
- Rome
- Britain

These are the societies that birthed Western culture, that odd set of ideas and values embraced by the peoples of Western Europe, North America, and Australia—those societies measured by the swinging of the Western Pendulum.

Zeniths of "We" in the Past Three Thousand Years

This is a list, on the following pages, of iconic persons and events that capture the spirit of the Zeniths of "We" for the past three thousand years. Many of the persons selected enjoyed a lifespan that touched both sides of the Pendulum. In these instances, the Upswing of "We" is that window of time in which they made their historic difference.

Figure 9.1 The Zenith of a "WE" Cycle.

The Law of Probability would tell us that an equal number of leaders working for the common good should be found at the Zeniths of "Me." Consequently, an honest skeptic reading this list of "We" Zeniths might assume that we have selected data to prove our assertions. Please be assured this is not the case; rather, we created this list by asking random experts to name the persons and events in history that best illustrate "working together for the common good." The persons polled had no clue how we planned to use the information.

We've listed all of the persons and events they named and added a few of our own because, frankly, even people well versed in history don't know much about the years 300 to 800 CE. We had to dig deep in these years to find historic examples of the "We," and frankly, the examples were hard to find. It's interesting to note, however, that every example of "We" thinking that we discovered in our research of the Dark Ages *occurred during the Upswing of a "We."* We didn't find a single example of "working together for the common good" in the Middle Ages that wasn't near the Zenith of a "We." Don't believe us? Investigate it for yourself. You'll find that what we say is true.

The twenty-year Upswing to a "We" Zenith happens only once every eighty years. This mean the statistical odds of an event happening in this window are only one in four.

WE   ZENITHS OF "WE" IN THE PAST 3,000 YEARS

937 BCE: ***Solomon,*** near the end of his life, learned the wisdom of serving others and told his story in the Bible's book of Ecclesiastes, written eight years before this Zenith of the "We." (Bible scholar Mark A. Copeland indicated that Solomon likely wrote the book of Ecclesiastes around 945 BCE, when he was sixty-six years old). Born in 1011 BCE, six years after a Zenith on the Downswing of a "We," Solomon's bar mitzvah happened just before the tipping point into the Upswing of a "Me." He was thirty-four years old at the "Me" Zenith (977 BCE) and fifty-four at the end of the "Me," when it reached the tipping point that took him into a new "We" that would Zenith in 937 BCE. He lived to be eighty years old. His Ecclesiastes is a very interesting book.

He wrote in the book of Ecclesiastes about his self-indulgence as a young man at the Zenith of a "Me":

I denied myself nothing my eyes desired; I refused my heart no pleasure. My heart took delight in all my labor, and this was the reward for all my toil.

—Ecclesiastes 2:10

He then explained what he learned during the Downswing of the "Me."

WE   Yet when I surveyed all that my hands had done and what I had toiled to achieve, everything was meaningless, a chasing after the wind; nothing was gained under the sun.

—Ecclesiastes 2:11

Read Ecclesiastes, and you'll experience the reflections of an old man who had lived through a "Me" and found it to be hollow. Ending his days in a "We," Solomon finally seemed to find the answers he sought:

WE I know that there is nothing better for people than to be happy and to do good while they live. That each of them may eat and drink, and find satisfaction in all their toil—this is the gift of God.

—Ecclesiastes 3:12–13

Solomon died in 931 BCE, six years after the Zenith of a "We," with society's Pendulum in precisely the same position it had been in when he was born. We'll take a second look at his life at the "Me" Zenith in another chapter.

---

857 BCE: Homer completes the *Iliad* and the *Odyssey* just seven years after this "We" Zenith (850 BCE). The oldest extant works of Western literature, these are considered fundamental to the modern Western canon and have been influential in shaping Western culture. Stories are written for unnamed and unseen others, not for oneself. Consequently, the creation of literature is one of the purest expressions of "We."

Capitoline Museum, Albani Collection

777 BCE: *The Olympic Games* were born in the year following this Zenith, according to the *Bibliotheca Historica* (Historical Library) of Diodorus Siculus, an ancient Greek historian. Modern scholars consider the date reliable. During a celebration of these ancient games an Olympic truce was enacted so that athletes could travel from their countries to the games in safety. As long as they met the entrance criteria, athletes from any country or city-state were allowed to participate. The prizes for the victors were olive wreaths or crowns.

---

697 BCE: *Hezekiah* ruled Judah in Israel, 726–697 BCE. (Other sources say his reign began in 715 BCE, but either way, his reign began during the Upswing of this "We.") To bring the people into unity, Hezekiah sent letters across Judah and Israel asking everyone to attend a Passover celebration. The event was a huge success: "There was great joy in Jerusalem, for since the days of Solomon son of David king of Israel there had been nothing like this in

Jerusalem."[1] Hezekiah strengthened Judah politically, expanded its borders, and built an underground tunnel to bring water into Jerusalem in case of a siege. Most scholars consider Hezekiah one of the best kings of any society in antiquity.

617 BCE: *Athenian Law* is codified by Draco, a legislator of ancient Athens, in 620 BCE, three years prior to the Zenith. Draco replaced the prevailing system of oral law delivered by *eupatrid thesmothetai*, "those who lay down the law," with a written code to be enforced only by a court. This was also about the time that Aesop was born in Greece. His fables would do much to accelerate the next "We" as it swung upward.

537 BCE: *Cyrus the Great* created the earliest known Bill of Rights in 539 BCE immediately following his conquest of Babylon. The document has been called "the first declaration of human rights, which, for its advocacy of humane principles, justice and liberty, must be considered one of the most remarkable documents in the history of mankind."[2] However, those who would prefer to disparage all things Persian have hotly contested this assessment. (Persia is current-day Iran.) It is notable, however, that this same Cyrus, according to the Bible, allowed the captive Jews to return to Jerusalem during the first year of his reign.[3]

457 BCE: *Decree of Artaxerxes I* reestablished the government of Jerusalem. Ezra, the author of the Old Testament book by the same name, spearheaded this effort. Nehemiah, the author of the Old Testament book by the same name and cupbearer to Artaxerxes I, was later sent to rebuild the city walls and restore its defenses.

377 BCE: *Plato* founded his Academy in Athens in 387 BCE, ten years prior to the Zenith of the "We." In approximately 380 BCE he wrote *The Republic*, his world-altering treatise that concluded that justice is better than injustice. Whether or not Plato arrived at the right answers is debatable, but most people throughout Western history have agreed that he definitely asked the right questions about how people should live.

297 BCE: *The "Latin Rights" Colony* of Carscoli is so designated by the Romans just one year prior to the Zenith of this "We." These Latin Rights are significant because an early Roman conqueror defeated this same Latin League in the Battle of Lake Regillus at the Zenith of a "Me" twenty years earlier. Rome, now in a "We," extended to these former enemies many of the privileges of Roman citizens, including the important rights of *commercium* (the right of transacting business and conducting lawsuits in Rome on the same footing as Roman citizens) and connubium (the right of intermarriage with Romans). In effect, Rome said, "We're willing to accept each of you into the group as one of us."

217 BCE: *The Roman Republic* chose to ignore its long-standing policy that soldiers must be both citizens and property owners. This opened the door for military service to the common man. This decision was made precisely at the Zenith of a "We." Meanwhile in Palestine, Rabbi Judah HaNasi coordinated the redaction of the oral Torah of Judaism during the Upswing of this "We" in order to form the Mishnah, thereby saving millennia of wisdom that otherwise would have been lost.

137 BCE: *Stoic Philosophy* arrived in Rome just three years prior to this Zenith of the "We." In that same year (140 BCE) playwright Lucius Accius has his first play, *Atreus,* performed in Rome. Most of his fifty plays are tragedies, of course, because whining about problems and sacrificing ourselves to make things better is what we do at the Zenith of a "We." Stoic Philosophy embraces the belief that pain and hardship should be endured without a display of feelings and without complaint, saying essentially, "Pain is good. Life is pain. Crap happens and then you die. But we are doing the right thing. Oh joy."

57 BCE: *Julius Caesar* (with Crassus and Pompey) used populist "We" tactics just three years prior to this Zenith to amass power within the Roman Senate. These tactics included feeding the poor (a grain dole) and limiting slavery, as slavery took jobs from poor free citizens. Caesar also garnered political support from the masses by attempting to expand citizenship to communities outside Italy.[4] Caesar later betrayed the "We" and used this power to make himself dictator-for-life. When he was assassinated for this "Me" ambition, society was still in a "We," although it was in the Downswing. Had Caesar made himself dictator during a "Me," he likely would not have been assassinated. His successor, Octavius, later to be called Caesar Augustus, became the first emperor of Rome in the Upswing of the following "Me" in 27 BCE, halfway to the Zenith.

Musée Arles antique

23: *Jesus* was presumably a carpenter in Nazareth at this time. Most scholars believe he was born between 6 BCE and 4 BCE, so he would have been around twenty-six to twenty-nine years old in 23 AD, when he was about to enter the wilderness for his forty-day fast. A new prefect of Judaea, Pontius Pilate, would be appointed three years later. Five years from then, Herod Antipas would execute John the Baptist, and shortly thereafter, in approximately 30 AD, Jesus would demonstrate the ultimate "We":

Greater love has no one than this: to lay down one's life for one's friends.

—*John 15:13*

103: *Pliny the Younger,* a consul of Rome, completed his *Panegyricus* and delivered it as oratory to the Roman Senate just three years prior to this Zenith of the "We." The *Panegyricus* describes in detail the actions of a good leader in fields of administrative power such as taxes, justice, military discipline, and commerce.[5] It served as something of a textbook for "We" administrations thereafter. It is notable that Pliny the Younger had been witness to the eruption of Mount Vesuvius twenty-one years earlier, in which his Uncle Pliny the Elder died.

183: *The Decline of the Roman Empire* begins in 180 AD following the death of Marcus Aurelius, the last of the "five good emperors," just three years prior to this Zenith. The current emperor is *Commodus,* an out-of-control ego who believes he is the reincarnation of Hercules, frequently emulating that legendary hero's feats by appearing in the Roman arena to fight a variety of wild animals. The absence of a dynamic "Me" leader forty years prior (at the Zenith of the "Me" of 143) had caused Rome to become unfocused and undergo an identity crisis. Remember: heroes strengthen the identity of a society.

Heroes raise the bar we jump and hold high the standards we live by. They are ever-present tattoos on our psyche, the embodiment of all we are striving to be. We create our heroes from our hopes and dreams. And then they attempt to create us in their own image.

—*"Monday Morning Memo," February 17, 2003*

Just ten years after this aborted "We" Zenith of 183 CE, a conspiracy of administrators near to Emperor Commodus sent his wrestling partner, Narcissus, to strangle Commodus in his bath, and that was the end of the reincarnated Hercules. The Senate of Rome would sentence the next emperor to death after he had ruled for only sixty-six days. When a committee can murder one emperor and vote death upon the next one, that society must not only be in a "We," but is likely floundering in the vacuum created by an absence of heroes.

WE A 'We' is about serving through small actions, but it has a dark side as well: we get tired of being good.

—*Michael R. Drew*

263: *Emperor Aurelian* built a wall around Rome (270) to protect the citizens from attack. To unify the people's religious beliefs, Aurelian chose to use the winter solstice to be celebrated as "The Birth of the Unconquered Sun." Roman Christians opted to embrace this celebration, but with a twist: they would celebrate a different birth. Later, Aurelian would be forgotten, but Christmas remained.

343: *Constantine the Great* of Rome sent grain, oil, iron, and wine to the Goths to thank them for repelling an invasion by the Vandals and Sarmatians. The Romans and the Goths then enter into a treaty. This was done in 331 AD, eight years after the tipping point on the Upswing of the "We."

Museo Chiaramonti

423: *Emperor Honorius* granted the title of "allies" to the Suevi/Asding Vandals [6]and gave the Visigoths the best land available in Gaul to settle upon (418). Also during the Upswing of this "We," the men who would become known as St. Jerome and St. Augustine of Hippo wrote "We" books that would influence the world for millennia.

503: *"Lex Romana Burgundionum,"* the Code introduced by *Gundobad,* King of Burgundy, gave rights to his Burgundian and Roman subjects alike. This was begun in 485, during the Upswing of this "We." In 493 Clotilda, the Burgundian princess, married Clovis and, having embraced the Roman Rite herself, helped convert Clovis to Roman Christianity. Clovis became the first ruler (481–511) of the Merovingian dynasty, a kingdom that stretched from Northern Spain to the feet of Norway and Sweden. Although Clovis wasn't a particularly great ruler, his conversion to Orthodox Christianity was enough to make him King of the Franks in the eyes of the pope.

583: *Peace Talks* between the Saxons and Celts were held shortly after this Zenith by the man who would become known as Saint Augustine of Canterbury. This effort began when Augustine traveled from Rome to Canterbury, the headquarters of the Saxon king Ethelbert. The Saxon people had a reputation for being barbaric and fierce.

663: *Augustine* wasn't completely successful in his peace talks eighty years earlier, but it is interesting to note that a meaningful peace between the Celts and the Saxons finally emerged precisely at this next Zenith of this "We."

743: *The Venerable Bede,* known as the father of English church history, spent the Upswing of this "We" making certain that future generations would have an accurate account of life in that place and time. *Bede was worried about people he would never meet.* He committed himself to benefiting all of society in a way that had no immediate benefit to himself. His most important book, *The Ecclesiastical History of the English People,* was written in 731. Forward-thinking actions for the benefit of all are typical during the Upswing of a "We."

823: *Charlemagne* ruled during the Upswing of this "We." The pope placed a gold crown on Charlemagne's head while he knelt in prayer at Saint Peter's on Christmas Day, 800 CE—the foundation of the Holy Roman Empire. Charlemagne believed the government should work to benefit those it ruled. He urged better farming methods and worked continually toward reforms that would improve the lives of the people. He even set up money standards to encourage commerce among the people. Charlemagne was not your average conqueror.

CC Image courtesy of Rama on Flickr

903: *Better education and social order* were the legacy of *Alfred the Great,* the Anglo-Saxon king during this Upswing of this "We." Alfred believed that learning "makes life more rewarding and enjoyable. . . . the worst thing of all is ignorance." His code of law based on the teachings of the Bible helped to maintain social order. He died in 899, just four years before the Zenith of this "We."

983: *Trial by Jury* was introduced by King Æthelred just fourteen years past this Zenith. Æthelred ruled England from 978 to 1016, with only a brief interruption in 1013 when Danish Viking raiders caused him to escape to Normandy for a year. Yes, they were perilous times—all the more reason to see his institution of trial by jury as remarkably advanced "We" thinking.

1063: *William the Conqueror* was crowned king on Christmas Day, 1066, at Westminster Abbey following the Battle of Hastings. William's only real distinction was that he commissioned the compilation of the *Domesday Book,* the precursor to the modern census, a survey of the productive capacity of the people of England.

1143: *Geoffrey of Monmouth* wrote *Historia Regum Britanniae* (*History of the Kings of Britain*) and, in so doing, created the legend of King Arthur and his *Knights of the Round Table,* men who sacrifice themselves willingly in the interest of doing good.

1223: *Magna Carta* was issued in 1215, eight years before the Zenith of this "We," and passed into law in 1225, two years after the Zenith. The Magna Carta was the first document forced onto an English King by a group of his subjects in an attempt to limit his powers by law. It is considered a precursor to the famous *"We the People . . ."* written by the framers of the US Constitution.

The Lateran Council of 1215 approved of burning at the stake as a punishment against heresy.

1303: *Carta Mercatoria* was issued by King Edward I. This allowed foreign merchants free entry and departure with their goods. Its message is that "A strong economy is the result of all of us working together."

1382: *Winchester College* was founded.[7] It is now over six hundred years old and is the oldest of the original nine schools defined by the English Public Schools Act of 1868. (Also among the nine were Eton, Harrow, and Charterhouse).[8] At about this same time King Richard II attempted to rule without consulting Parliament. The forces of the Lords Appellant quickly overpowered Richard's small army outside Oxford, and he was imprisoned in the Tower of London until he apologized and promised not to do it again.

1463: *Thomas Malory, just seven years after this Zenith,* completed his own version of the resurrected stories that had been told by Geoffrey of Monmouth 320 years earlier. Malory's tales of the Knights of the Round Table and their deeds for society glisten once more in his *Le Morte d'Arthur.* It is notable that the

The Boy's King Arthur: "Sir Mador's spear brake all to pieces, but the other's spear held.

technological "We" *Alpha Voice* that emerged shortly before the Upswing of "We" is the printing press of Johann Gutenberg. Wikipedia reports that printing presses in Western Europe produced more than twenty million books by the year 1500. A single Renaissance printing press could produce thirty-six hundred pages per workday.[9] Consequently, books by best-selling authors, such as Martin Luther, were sold by the hundreds of thousands in their lifetime.

1543: *Copernicus* announced that the Earth is not the center of the universe but that it, in fact, revolves around the Sun. It stands to reason that this realization and the subsequent announcement that "We are not the center of the universe" would be made at the Zenith of a "We." Can you imagine anyone coming to that conclusion during a "Me"?

Just eleven years past this "We" Zenith, England's "Bloody Mary" revived the practice of burning at the stake and offers 284 Protestants as her offering to God.

1623: *The English Petition of Right* stipulated that the king could no longer tax without Parliament's permission. This was passed in 1628, just five years after the Zenith. In 1624, just one year beyond the Zenith, the following words were written:

WE No man is an island, entire of itself; every man is a piece of the continent, a part of the main. If a clod be washed away by the sea, Europe is the less as well as if a promontory were, as well as if a manor of thy friend's or of thine own were: Any man's death diminishes me, because I am involved in mankind; and therefore never send to know for whom the bell tolls; it tolls for thee.[10]

—*John Donne, Meditation XVII*

1703: *The English Bill of Rights* provided freedom of speech and banned cruel or unusual punishment. These strengthened Parliament further and gave the people more rights to express themselves. It was passed in 1689 during the Upswing of a "We," of course. This Upswing of the "We" (1683 1703) includes the *Glorious Revolution* (1688–1689) that established the final victory of Parliament (We) over the king (Me).

The Salem Witch Trials of 1692 began just eleven years prior to this "We" Zenith, making burning at the stake popular once more.

1783: *The United States won the Revolutionary War* and the US Congress ratified a preliminary peace treaty with Britain. British troops left New York City. In just three more years America's founding document would open with the words, *"We the People . . ."* One of the great "We" documents of all time, the US Constitution was written on the Upswing of a "We," of course. Just six years after this Zenith, the last article of *Declaration of the Rights of Man and of the Citizen* was adopted (August 1789) by the National Constituent Assembly of France (Assemblée nationale constituante) during the French Revolution.

1863: *Gettysburg Address,* in which Abraham Lincoln stated, "Four score and seven years ago our fathers brought forth on this continent a new nation, conceived in liberty, and *dedicated to the proposition that all men are created equal."* Just two years later, in 1865, French law professor and politician Édouard René de Laboulaye, a supporter of the Union in the American Civil War, made a comment during after-dinner conversation at his home near Versailles, stating, "If a monument should rise in the United States, as a memorial to their independence, I should think it only natural if it were built by united effort—a common work of both our nations." Laboulaye's comment was not intended as a proposal, but nonetheless it inspired a young sculptor, Frédéric Bartholdi, who was present at the dinner.[11] Bartholdi then went on to sculpt the *Statue of Liberty* and arranged for it to be given as a gift to America. Emma Lazarus later wrote the poem we all

CC Image courtesy of Wknight94 on Flickr

know, whose lines include, "Give me your tired, your poor, your huddled masses yearning to breathe free, the wretched refuse of your teeming shore. Send these, the homeless, tempest-tost to me, I lift my lamp beside the golden door!"

1943: *Adolph Hitler* was the German promoter of "I'm OK, you're *not* OK," 1933–1945. Joseph Stalin was the Soviet promoter during his "Great Purge" of 1936–1938. Senator Joseph McCarthy was the American witch-hunt specialist with the help of the "Un-American Activities Committee," 1937–1953.

Union membership and military enlistments reached an all-time high in the United States. In Germany, nationalism was surging, as Germans began burning books at the halfway point of the Upswing. Sigmund Freud's books were prominent among those they burned, to which he quipped, "What progress we are making! In the Middle Ages they would have burned me. Now, they are content with burning my books." In 1938, five years before the

Zenith, T. H. White's *The Sword in the Stone* was published, the first volume in the eventual quartet of books published as *The Once and Future King*, White's version of Malory's version of the Knights of the Round Table. Just two years before this "We" Zenith, John Steinbeck mocked the dreams and illusions that are part of every "Me":

WE There is a story told of a Swedish tramp, sitting in a ditch on midsummer night. He was ragged and dirty, and drunk, and he said to himself softly and in wonder, "I am rich, and happy, and perhaps a little beautiful."

—from Sea of Cortez[12]

The Story of King Arthur and His Knights © Howard Pyle

Approaching this Zenith of the "We," John Steinbeck wrote his first commercial success, *Tortilla Flat,* which he considered to be a contemporary retelling of the story of the Knights of the Round Table. This is thus the *third* time that story has showed up at the Zenith of a "We," and this time it showed up *twice*.

2023: *Wait and see.* Or if you're really curious, keep reading and see what the authors are predicting. (Frankly, if you're not anticipating a resurgence of interest in the story of the Knights of the Round Table, we can only assume you've not been paying attention).

A "We" is about serving through small actions, but it has a dark side as well: *we get tired of being good.* The actions we once took willingly begin to lose their sparkle, until finally the chains of duty, obligation, and sacrifice bind us. Although we are self-righteous and proud in our service to others, secretly, it dissatisfies us. We begin to long for the freedom and rewards and dizzying heights of "Me." Near the pinnacle of the 1943 "We," a famous novelist made the following observation:

WE There is a strange duality in the human which makes for an ethical paradox. We have definitions of good qualities and of bad. Of the good, we always think of wisdom, tolerance, kindliness, generosity, humility; and the qualities of cruelty, greed, self-interest, graspingness, and rapacity are universally considered undesirable. And yet in our structure of society, the so-called and considered good qualities are invariable concomitants of failure, while the bad ones are the cornerstones of success. A man—a viewing-point man—while he will love the abstract good qualities and detest the abstract bad, will nevertheless envy and admire the person who through possessing the abstract bad qualities has succeeded economically and socially, and will hold in contempt that person whose good qualities have caused failure. When such a viewing-point man considers Jesus or St. Augustine or Socrates he regards them with love because they are the symbols of the good he admires, and he hates the symbols of the bad. But actually he would rather be successful than good.

—*John Steinbeck, Sea of Cortez*[13]

Near the Zenith of the most recent "Me," women had big hair, cars were dramatic two-tone affairs, and kids were killed for their tennis shoes, as though they thought, *I must own those shoes. I have no status without them.*

iStockphoto / Alina555

Conversely, near the Zenith of a "We," personal liberties are stripped away for the common good: "Do you recycle? You should. You're not on this planet alone." "Secondhand smoke is like a drive-by shooting. If you don't care about your own health, you should at least care about the health of the children who breathe what you exhale." "Your hybrid vehicle still burns gasoline, you know. If you really cared about the planet you'd ride a bike."

PAPER   GLASS   PLASTIC   METAL

iStockphoto / onurdongel

Yes, we always carry a good thing too far. In the upper reaches of a "We," the once-beautiful dream of connectedness and working together for the common good slowly degenerates into a series of restrictions that make us feel righteous. This righteous momentum carries us into duty, obligation, and sacrifice long after the dream is over.

And now we understand why, in 1898, George Bernard Shaw quoted Shakespeare: "When a stupid man is doing something he is ashamed of, he always declares that it is his duty."[14]

As Shaw approached the "Me" Zenith of 1903, he was ridiculing the legalism and restrictiveness of the "We" in which he had grown up. Ten years later, at the halfway point of the Downswing from that same "Me," Henry Ford's 1913 introduction of the first assembly line that employed conveyor belts was an Alpha Voice of technology that gave us a glimpse of the "We" thinking that would become mainstream in 1923.

But as we've already looked at the "We" Upswing of 1923 to 1943, let's now take a look at the Downswing from that Zenith.

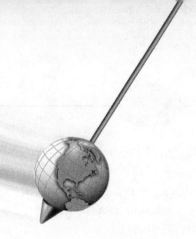

Pendulum Legend

The Downswing of a "We" is when we exhale from the emotional exhaustion
that comes from trying so very hard to be "good."

CHAPTER TEN

1943–1953:
The First Half of the
Downswing of "We"

Chin up, head high, and proud, we encourage one another to "do the right thing" during the Downswing of "We," but we are also weary and worn. It is a time of duty, obligation, and sacrifice. Regimentation has replaced inspiration, process smothers innovation, and policy precludes personal judgment.

The Downswing of a "We" is when we exhale from the emotional exhaustion that comes from trying so very hard to be "good."

Pulled by the gravity of the Moon, the rise and fall of the tide is a reliable phenomenon in every large body of water on our planet.

Figure 10.1   The first half of a downswing of "WE."

Likewise, the social trends the Pendulum measures are immutable. But these trends have long escaped our notice because, unlike the twenty-four-hour cycle of the tide, a complete cycle of the Pendulum is eighty years.

The Granger Collection, NYC

Born Yesterday was the 1946 hit play on Broadway that openly mocked the "Me" perspective. In it, wealthy and powerful Harry Brock makes a trip to Washington, DC, to buy a senator. Harry is loud and domineering. The play revolves around his girlfriend, Billie Dawn. "I started in thinking," she says, "I couldn't get to sleep for ten minutes." Dawn is clearly an ignoramus, but without shame. She says to her tutor, Paul Verrall, who has been hired to educate her so that she can blend into Washington society, "I'm stupid, and I like it," though he dissuades this attitude. Under his tutelage, the bimbo becomes a bookworm. Critic John Lahr for the *New Yorker* stated,

> **WE** Billie's transformation acts out on a personal level the public awakening for which the play argues—the shedding of corrupt laissez-faire attitudes for more responsible social policy.[1]

Born Yesterday opened on February 4, 1946, and ran for 1,642 performances. It was then adapted into a 1950 film for which Judy Holliday won an Oscar for best actress. In the words of Lahr, the play is a theatrical argument for "the shedding of corrupt laissez-faire attitudes for more responsible social policy." Is it any wonder *Born Yesterday* was revived on Broadway in 2011, when society was again approaching the Zenith of a "We"?

Figure 10.2 *Characteristics of society at the Zenith of a "WE" cycle.*

WE	ZENITH CHARACTERISTICS

TAKING A GOOD THING TOO FAR

"WHEN A STUPID MAN IS DOING SOMETHING HE IS ASHAMED OF, HE ALWAYS DECLARES THAT IT IS HIS DUTY."—George Bernard Shaw

• Personal liberties stripped away	• Long for freedom
• Self-righteous	• Regimentation
• Duty, obligation, sacrifice	• Process smothers innovation
• Secretly dissatisfied	• Claustrophobic and oppressive

Music

Let's look now at the values reflected in popular music during the Downswing from the "We" of 1943. Notice how the lyrics of the number-one hits reflect the hunger of unmet needs while at the same time encouraging the public to "do the right thing."

Figure 10.3 *Popular music themes after a "WE" Zenith.*

WE POPULAR MUSIC THEMES: FIRST HALF OF A DOWNSWING FROM "WE" (1943–1953)

A TIME OF DUTY, OBLIGATION, AND SACRIFICE

1944: "Swinging on a Star," Bing Crosby MESSAGE

And by the way, if you hate to go to school
You may grow up to be a mule.

Do the right thing or you'll suffer.

The Granger Collection, NYC

1945: "Sentimental Journey," Les Brown	MESSAGE

Gonna take a sentimental journey,
to renew old memories.

Yesterday was better than this.

1946: "Prisoner of Love," Perry Como

Although she has another,
I can't have another, for I'm not free!"

I want something I can't have.

1947: "Chi-Baba, Chi-Baba," Perry Como

Many a year ago in old Sorrento a certain ditty was
    quite the thing,
Whenever a mother rocked her baby in Sorrento this little
    ditty she used to sing

Yesterday was beautiful.

1948: "Buttons and Bows," Dinah Shore

My bones denounce the buckboard bounce
And the cactus hurts my toes

**I'm tired of plain things! Give
me finery!**

1949: "Ghost Riders in the Sky," Vaughn Monroe

If you want to save your soul from hell a' ridin' on our range
Then, cowboy, change your ways today

Do the right thing or you'll suffer.

1950: "Mona Lisa," Nat King Cole

Do you smile to tempt a lover, Mona Lisa?
Or is this your way to hide a broken heart?

MESSAGE

What I desire seems distant from me.

CC Image

Pendulum Legend

The Alpha Voices of literature often pay a heavy price for their immortality: Salinger went into deep seclusion for the rest of his life and Kerouac drank himself to death.

—*Michael R. Drew*

CHAPTER ELEVEN

1953–1963:
The Second Half of the
Downswing of "We"

Figure 11.1 The second half of a downswing of "WE."

Figure 11.2 Mindset and values of a "ME" mindset.

MINDSET	ME

BE #1. SECOND PLACE IS THE FIRST LOSER.

Values	Rejects
• Big dreams	• Small actions
• Individual expression	• Conformity
• Freedom	• Self-sacrifice
• Feeling good, looking good	• Self-denial
• Personal achievement	• Personal responsibility
• Rose-colored lenses	• Reality check

Figure 11.3 Alpha voices leading into a "ME" cycle.

ALPHA VOICES LEADING INTO A "ME" (1953–1963)	ME

Literature: Charles Baudelaire's poems republished.	MESSAGE: Reckless, uninhibited heroes
Playboy makes its debut.	breaking free from restraints of polite
J. D. Salinger writes *Catcher in the Rye*	society are what we want. Flaunt
Jack Kerouac writes *On the Road*	your freedom.
Technology: The first Corvette	MESSAGE: Whoever drives me is free to
	be young, free, and beautiful forever
	Life is an adventure. Hop in.
Music: Rock and Roll is born	MESSAGE: Loosen up and move around. It's not
	obscene—it feels good and it's fun!

In the second half of the weary Downswing of a "We," doubts and second thoughts begin to whisper, "Why are we doing all this?"

Although Charles Baudelaire died in 1867, his republished poems became an Alpha Voice that inspired a weary "beat" generation in 1953, halfway down a "We," when society had pushed its dream of "working together for the common good" all the way to social obligation and halfway back down again. Under the weary, gray sky of the thirtieth year of "We," the Alpha Voices of "Me" created a tropical island in the mind.

ME And if sometimes you wake up, on palace steps, on the green grass of a ditch, in your room's gloomy solitude, your intoxication already waning or gone, ask the wind, the waves, the stars, the birds, the clocks, ask everything that flees, everything that moans, everything that moves, everything that sings, everything that speaks, ask what time it is. And the wind, the waves, the stars, the birds, clocks, will answer, "It is time to get high! So as not to be martyred slaves of Time, get high; get high constantly! On wine, on poetry, or on virtue, as you wish."[1]

Charles Baudelaire's republished one-hundred–year-old poems ignited our long-suppressed hunger for a little "me time" in 1953. Interestingly, Baudelaire was born in 1821, just two years before the Zenith of a "Me," so that "Me" perspective (1823–1843) would have informed his earliest values. Sadly, the tipping point into "We" came when he was just twenty-two, so Baudelaire became an out-of-step, countercultural, minority "Me" voice in  French literature during the Upswing of that "We" to its Zenith (1843–1863).

So outraged was French society at what Baudelaire had written that he, his publisher, and even the printer were successfully prosecuted for creating an offense against public morals.[2] Nearly one hundred years later, on May 11, 1949, during the Downswing of a "We" back toward a "Me" again, Baudelaire was vindicated, the judgment against him was officially reversed, and his banned poems were reinstated in France. Unfortunately, he was dead.

1953: Alpha Voices in Technology, Halfway Down the "We."

Cars: In 1953 they are heavy, bloated, and butt-ugly. But guess what arrives on the scene this year? *The very first Corvette!* And every one

of them is a convertible. The message of that car was clear: "Whoever drives me is going to be young and free and beautiful forever, the sun shining always on them, and the wind blowing through their hair. Who needs a roof when it's never going to rain? Who needs a backseat? 'Me Tarzan, you Jane,' and the open road are all that matter. Pull up to the curb alongside her, swing open the door, and say, 'Life is an adventure, girl. Hop in.'"

Literature: *Playboy* made its debut in 1953 with a naked Marilyn Monroe on the cover of issue number one. Society gasped and was embarrassed, never suspecting that "free love" would be the mantra of its heroes in just a few more years.

The books that emerged during this Alpha window showed us reckless, uninhibited heroes who broke free from the constraints of polite society and flaunted their freedoms in the face of whoever might be watching. Baudelaire lives again.

Remember Sal Paradise and Dean Moriarty in Jack Kerouac's thinly disguised diary of his cross-country journey with Neal Cassady, *On the Road*? Remember Holden Caulfield of J. D. Salinger's *Catcher in the Rye*?

Each of these tormented, self-willed heroes made our eyes pop open as we gasped, "He's a wild man! He does whatever he wants and doesn't worry about the consequences! He doesn't obey the rules!"

Kerouac's Sal Paradise said,

The Granger Collection, NYC

ME As the cab honked outside and the kids cried and the dogs barked and Dean danced with Frankie, I yelled every conceivable curse I could think over that phone and added all kinds of new ones, and in my drunken frenzy I told everybody over the phone to go to hell and slammed it down and went out to get drunk.[3]

Salinger's Holden Caulfield says, "Sleep tight, ya morons!"; "Goddam money. It always ends up making you blue as hell"; and "I hate actors. They never act like people. They just think they do."[4]

We had never read anything like these books, so we purchased three million copies of Kerouac's book and sixty-five million of Salinger's and then found a young man named James Dean to play this tormented, reckless, and self-willed hero in a movie called *Rebel without a Cause*. Dean played this same character twice more in *East of Eden* and *Giant* before driving his Porsche Spyder into a head-on collision at the age of twenty-four.

Jack Kerouac's *Belief and Technique for Modern Prose* gives us a sense of how it feels when an Alpha Voice of "Me" begins to whisper in the ear of a been-doing-the right-thing-for-way-too-long "We."

1. Scribbled secret notebooks, and wild typewritten pages, for your own joy
2. Submissive to everything, open, listening
3. Try never get drunk outside yr own house
4. Be in love with yr life
5. Something that you feel will find its own form
6. Be crazy dumbsaint of the mind
7. Blow as deep as you want to blow
8. Write what you want bottomless from bottom of the mind
9. The unspeakable visions of the individual
10. No time for poetry but exactly what is
11. Visionary tics shivering in the chest
12. In tranced fixation dreaming upon object before you
13. Remove literary, grammatical, and syntactical inhibition
14. Like Proust be an old teahead of time

15. Telling the true story of the world in interior monolog

16. The jewel center of interest is the eye within the eye

17. Write in recollection and amazement for yourself

18. Work from pithy middle eye out, swimming in language sea

19. Accept loss forever

20. Believe in the holy contour of life

21. Struggle to sketch the flow that already exists intact in mind

22. Don't think of words when you stop but to see picture better

23. Keep track of every day the date emblazoned in your morning

24. No fear or shame in the dignity of yr experience, language & knowledge

25. Write for the world to read and see yr exact pictures of it

26. Bookmovie is the movie in words, the visual American form

27. In praise of Character in the Bleak inhuman Loneliness

28. Composing wild, undisciplined, pure, coming in from under, crazier the better

29. You're a Genius all the time

30. Writer-Director of Earthly movies Sponsored & Angeled in Heaven[5]

Unable to reconcile himself to the "Me Generation" that blossomed all around him, Kerouac drank himself to death. These are the opening lines of his obituary in the *New York Times,* just twelve years after his book shook us like an earthquake.

ME Jack Kerouac, Novelist, Dead; Father of the Beat Generation: Author of *On the Road* was Hero to Youth—Rejected Middle-Class Values

Jack Kerouac, the novelist who named the Beat Generation and exuberantly celebrated its rejection of middle-class American conventions, died early yesterday of massive abdominal hemorrhaging in a St. Petersburg, Fla., hospital. He was 47 years old.

"The only people for me are the mad ones, the ones who are mad to live, mad to talk, desirous of everything at the same time," he wrote in *On the Road,* a novel he completed in only three weeks but had to wait seven years to see published.

When it finally appeared in 1957, it immediately became a basic text for youth who found their country claustrophobic and oppressive.[6]

Kerouac's *On the Road* became the bible of the Beats, later to be called the Beatniks, who in just eight short years would evolve into the Hippies.

But according to Kerouac's authorized biographer, historian Douglas Brinkley, *On the Road* was misinterpreted as a tale of companions out looking for kicks, "but the most important thing to comprehend is that Kerouac was an American Catholic author."[7] Kerouac was trying to make everything holy. The very term 'beat,' for 'Beatitude of Christ' kind of came to Kerouac at a Catholic church. And when I edited his diaries, really almost every page, he drew a crucifix or a prayer to God, or asking Christ for forgiveness.

Yes, the Alpha Voices of literature often pay a heavy price for their immortality: Salinger went into deep seclusion for the rest of his life, and Kerouac drank himself to death.

But notice how the number-one song of 1953 is very similar to the songs of the previous thirty years. Literature and technology are whispering of changes to come, but not music—not yet.

1953: Song of the Year: "Vaya con Dios" ("May God Be with You"), Les Paul and Mary Ford	MESSAGE
Now the time has come to part, The time for wee ping.	"I'm sad because I don't have what I want.

As 1953 spiraled toward 1958, a new musical genre, rock and roll, was born. No one knew quite what to think of it. Was it dirty and inappropriate, or was it lighthearted and free? The TV networks were so unsure how to handle it, they would show only the upper body of Elvis "the Pelvis" Presley on national TV. The public was simultaneously titillated and repulsed, fascinated and confused.

Just six months prior to the beginning of 1958, a young crooner said,

WE They are way off-base with their onstage contortions. I don't think anything excuses the suggestive gyrations that some rock-and-rollers go in for.... I belong to the finger-snapping school myself. That, and a little tapping of the feet, is enough to satisfy my soul. And it seems to satisfy my audiences, too.

—*Pat Boone, This Week, July 7, 1957*

Bibliothèque nationale de France

Frank Sinatra, the king of the crooners, declared, "Boone is better than Elvis. He has better technique and can sing several types of songs. He's the one who will last longer."[8]

Although rock and roll wasn't yet the choice of the mainstream majority, we were were not yet at the tipping point either. Indeed, most of the top-twenty songs for 1958 sounded similar to the whining crooners of previous years, but take a look at number four and seventeen—*rock and roll*.

A solid thirty of the Top 100 embrace the upbeat, new "Me" outlook called rock and roll, and another dozen songs lean gently toward it while keeping the other foot planted safely in crooner whine.

WE	ME
1. **"Tom Dooley,"** The Kingston Trio	MESSAGE
Hang down your head, Tom Dooley Hang down your head and cry Hang down your head, Tom Dooley Poor boy, you're bound to die.	**Do the wrong thing and you'll suffer for it.**
2. **"All I Have to Do Is Dream,"** The Everly Brothers	
3. **"Volare,"** Domenico Modugno	
4. **"Johnny B. Goode,"** Chuck Berry—*rock and roll!*	
Maybe someday your name will be in lights Saying "Johnny B. Goode tonight."	**You've got talent and you're going to be famous!**
5. **"Bird Dog,"** The Everly Brothers	
6. **"Tequila,"** Champs	
7. **"It's All in the Game,"** Tommy Edwards	
8. **"It's Only Make Believe,"** Conway Twitty	
9. **"When,"** The Kalin Twins	
10. **"Who's Sorry Now?"** Connie Francis	
11. **"Patricia,"** Perez Prado	
12. **"Twilight Time,"** The Platters	
13. **"Summertime Blues,"** Eddie Cochran	
14. **"Yakety Yak,"** The Coasters—*rock and roll!*	

15. **"Catch a Falling Star,"** Perry Como

16. **"La Bamba,"** Ritchie Valens—*rock and roll!*

17. **"One Night,"** Elvis Presley—*rock and roll!*

18. **"Fever,"** Peggy Lee

19. **"Witch Doctor,"** David Seville & the Chipmunks—*rock and roll!*

20. **"Sweet Little Sixteen,"** Chuck Berry—*rock and roll!*

21. **"I Got Stung,"** Elvis Presley—*rock and roll!*

22. **"Don't,"** Elvis Presley—*rock and roll!*

23. **"Volare,"** Dean Martin

24. **"Little Star,"** Elegants

25. **"Sail along Silvery Moon,"** Billy Vaughn

26. **"Magic Moments,"** Perry Como

27. **"Get a Job,"** The Silhouettes—*rock and roll!*

28. **"To Know Him is to Love Him,"** The Teddy Bears

29. **"Hard Headed Woman,"** Elvis Presley—*rock and roll!*

30. **"Good Golly Miss Molly!"** Little Richard—*rock and roll!*

31. **"Chantilly Lace,"** Big Bopper—*rock and roll!*

32. **"Poor Little Fool,"** Ricky Nelson—*rock and roll!*

33. **"He's Got the Whole World in His Hands,"** Laurie London

34. **"Return to Me,"** Dean Martin

Library of Congress

35. **"Lollipop,"** The Chordettes—*rock and roll!*

36. **"Rockin' Robin,"** Bobby Day—*rock and roll!*

37. **"Stupid Cupid,"** Connie Francis—*rock and roll!*

38. **"Wear My Ring around Your Neck,"** Elvis Presley—*rock and roll!*

39. **"Purple People Eater,"** Sheb Wooley—*rock and roll!*

40. **"C'mon Everybody,"** Eddie Cochran—*rock and roll!*

41. **"Lonely Teardrops,"** Jackie Wilson

42. **"Rumble,"** Link Wray

43. **"Tears on My Pillow,"** The Imperials

44. **"I Wonder Why,"** Dion & the Belmonts

45. **"Rave On,"** Buddy Holly—*rock and roll!*

46. **"Do You Want to Dance?"** Bobby Freeman—*rock and roll!*

47. **"Rebel Rouser,"** Duane Eddy—*rock and roll!*

48. **"The Story of My Life,"** Michael Holliday

49. **"You Are My Destiny,"** Paul Anka

50. **"The Day the Rains Came,"** Jane Morgan

51. **"Sixteen Candles,"** The Crests

52. **"Stood Up,"** Ricky Nelson

53. **"Buona Sera,"** Louis Prima

54. **"King Creole,"** Elvis Presley—*rock and roll!*

55. **"Carolina Moon,"** Connie Francis

56. **"March from the River Kwai,"** Mitch Miller

57. **"The Chipmunk Song (Christmas Don't Be Late),"** David Seville & the Chipmunks

58. **"Splish Splash,"** Bobby Darin

59. **"A Pub with No Beer,"** Slim Dusty

60. **"Guaglione,"** Perez Prado

61. **"Tea for Two,"** Tommy Dorsey

62. **"Maybe,"** The Chantels

63. **"Claudette,"** Everly Brothers

64. **"For Your Precious Love,"** Jerry Butler

65. **"My True Love,"** Jack Scott

66. **"Susie Darlin',"** Robin Luke

67. **"Devoted to You,"** The Everly Brothers

68. **"La Paloma,"** Billy Vaughn

69. **"Move It,"** Cliff Richard

70. **"Breathless,"** Jerry Lee Lewis—*rock and roll!*

71. **"Mandolins in the Moonlight,"** Perry Como

72. **"A Certain Smile,"** Johnny Mathis

73. **"Hoots Mon,"** Lord Rockingham's XI

74. **"More Than Ever,"** Coma Prima

75. **"Whole Lotta Woman,"** Marvin Rainwater

76. **"Book of Love,"** The Monotones—*rock and roll!*

77. **"Queen of the Hop,"** Bobby Darin

78. **"Gotta Travel On,"** Billy Grammer

79. **"Rock 'n' Roll Is Here to Stay,"** Danny & the Juniors—*rock and roll!*

80. **"One for My Baby,"** Shirley Bassey

81. **"As I Love You,"** Shirley Bassey

82. **"Big Man,"** Four Preps

83. **"Problems,"** The Everly Brothers

84. **"Whole Lotta Loving,"** Fats Domino—*rock and roll!*

85. **"A Lover's Question,"** Clyde McPhatter

86. **"High School Confidential,"** Jerry Lee Lewis—*rock and roll!*

87. **"Willie & the Hand Jive,"** Johnny Otis—*rock and roll!*

88. **"Carol,"** Chuck Berry—*rock and roll!*

89. **"Born Too Late,"** Poni-Tails

90. **"Crazy Love,"** Paul Anka

91. **"Witchcraft,"** Frank Sinatra

92. **"Try Me,"** James Brown—*rock and roll!*

93. **"Come Prima,"** Dalida

94. **"Goodbye Baby,"** Jack Scott

National Archives and Records Administration

95. **"Western Movies,"** Olympics

96. **"Lonesome Town,"** Ricky Nelson

97. **"A Wonderful Time Up There,"** Pat Boone

98. **"Short Shorts,"** Royal Teens

99. **"Maybe Baby,"** Buddy Holly—*rock and roll!*

100. **"Tulips from Amsterdam,"** Max Bygraves

Two years later we elected a good-looking young president with a pretty wife, and on May 25, 1961, just prior to the tipping point into a new "Me," President John F. Kennedy addressed a special joint session of Congress with these words:

 I believe that this nation should commit itself to achieving the goal, before this decade is out, of landing a man on the Moon and returning him safely to the Earth. No single space project in this period will be more impressive to mankind. . . .

Essentially, we said, "Let's go to the Moon!"
"Why?"
"Because we can do anything! Youth! Beauty! Vitality! Energy! Nothing can stop us!"

 Go-go-go Johnny,
Go. Go.
—Johnny B. Goode

But Dr. Albert Schweitzer, one of the last great voices of the fading "We" said,

 In the hopes of reaching the Moon, men fail to see the flowers that blossom at their feet.[9]

With society rushing ever more quickly toward the tipping point, aviator Anne Morrow Lindbergh wrote, "America, which has the most glorious present still existing in the world today, hardly stops to enjoy it, in her insatiable appetite for the future."[10]

So individuality and freedom of expression are paramount in a "Me," whereas working together for the common good is paramount in a "We."

"Me" and "We"—both are beautiful, but each have a dark side. The "Me," like the gravity of the moon, creates tides of pride that rise higher and higher. The "We," like the momentum of water, creates waves of polarity that crash upon the shores of society. The key to riding the waves is to understand the forces that move the masses and know approximately when a society will reverse and head back the other direction.

Pendulum Legend

Welcome to the Upswing of "Me," when individualism is the holy grail
of human existence and everyone asks, "Who am I?" and wonders,
"Am I being true to myself?"

CHAPTER TWELVE

1963–1973:
The First Half of the
Upswing into "Me"

In the early years of an Upswing, life is beautiful and anything is possible.

 If you look at the history of youth cultural movements, they tend to go one of two ways. One is in the direction of individual expression and creativity; the best example is the '60s. The other way is to lose themselves in the collective, binding themselves into a gang.

—*Jaron Lanier*[1]

Figure 12.1   The first half of the upswing to "ME."

Rita Mae Brown was born November 28, 1944, so she was eighteen when the big ball fell in New York's Times Square and 1963 began. A clear "Me" voice crying out for individuality, Rita Mae said, "The reward for conformity is that everyone likes you but yourself." She then went on to say,

ME Lead me not into temptation; I can find the way myself. Good judgment comes from experience, and often experience comes from bad judgment.

A life of reaction is a life of slavery, intellectually and spiritually. One must fight for a life of action, not reaction.

About all you can do in life is be who you are. Some people will love you for you. Most will love you for what you can do for them, and some won't like you at all.

What's the point of being a lesbian if a woman is going to look and act like an imitation man?

Welcome to the Upswing of "Me," when individualism is the holy grail of human existence and everyone asks, "Who am I?" and wonders, "Am I being true to myself?" Bob Dylan calmly assured us that "The answer, my friend, is blowin' in the wind. The answer is blowin' in the wind."

Figure 12.2 Characteristics of "ME."

CHARACTERISTICS OF "ME"	ME

1. Freedom of expression
2. Personal liberty
3. One man is wiser than a million men.
4. Wants to achieve a better life—"I came, I saw, I conquered."
5. Big dreams
6. Wants to be number one
7. Individual confidence and decisive persons
8. Leadership is "Look at me. Admire me. Emulate me if you can."
9. Elevates attractive heroes to strengthen society's sense of identity

The only people for me are the mad ones, the ones who are mad to live, mad to talk, mad to be saved, desirous of everything at the same time, the ones who never yawn or say a commonplace thing, but burn, burn, burn, like fabulous yellow Roman candles exploding like spiders across the stars, and in the middle, you see the blue center-light pop, and everybody goes "Awww!"

—Jack Kerouac, On the Road

We told you Eeyore the Donkey from Disney's *Winnie-the-Pooh* would be the perfect spokesperson for a "We." Eeyore sighs deeply and, effectively, says, "Somebody's got to do it, and it's probably me. Oh, well. Let's get started."

But the spokesperson for "Me" is Tigger. When Tigger introduces himself, he makes sure you understand that he is spontaneous, light-hearted, carefree, and reckless,

 But the most wonderful thing about tiggers is . . . *I'm the only one!*

A "Me" is all about individuality. Right on schedule at the tipping point, the Corvette got a whole new look. The '63 Stingray "split-window coupe" is the most rare and exotic Corvette of them all.

A woman from L'Oréal looked out from our televisions and told us that she colors her hair "Because I'm worth it."

"Me" looks for pleasure and status: identify beauty, focus on it, celebrate the moment and experience joy.

"Me" anticipates future pleasures and ignores the long-term consequences of present actions. "Me" is about sensation by every definition of the word.

1963: "Louie, Louie," The Kingsmen	MESSAGE
A fine little girl, she waits for me.	**I'm looking forward to being**
Me catch a ship across the sea.	**with the girl I love.**
Me sail the ship all alone;	
Me never think I make it home.	

Figure 12.3 *"ME" Mindset*

"ME" MINDSET	ME
LIFE IS BEAUTIFUL AND ANYTHING IS POSSIBLE IN THE EARLY YEARS OF AN UPSWING	

Individuality	Carefree
Spontaneous	Reckless
Lighthearted	Sensation

WE SPOKESPERSON	ME SPOKESPERSON
Eeyore	Tigger
Somebody's got to do it. And it's probably me.	*But the most wonderful thing about*
Oh well. Let's get started.	*Tiggers is . . . I'm the only one!*

Written in the style of a Jamaican ballad, "Louie, Louie" feels as though it were written by someone who had just read the thirty essential tips of Jack Kerouac's *Belief and Technique for Modern Prose*.

Because this was only the first year following the tipping point, society still had plenty of uptight people clinging to the comfort of legalism. In February, 1964, an outraged parent wrote to the US Attorney General alleging that the lyrics of "Louie, Louie" were obscene,[2] claiming that the lyrics said,

 A fine little bitch, she waits for me;
She gets her kicks on top of me.
Each night I take her out all alone;
She ain't the kind I lay at home.

In response, J. Edgar Hoover instructed the FBI to obtain a copy of the recording and, after a thirty-one-month investigation, they concluded that the lyrics were "unintelligible at any speed" and, therefore, the recording could not be obscene.

Robert Stone, author of *Prime Green: Remembering the Sixties*, remembers sitting and talking with Ken Kesey, the author who made his name with *One Flew Over the Cuckoo's Nest* (1962) and would later become the central character in Tom Wolfe's *The Electric Kool-Aid Acid Test* (1968).

ME [I]t was good to be alive and to be young was even better. More than the inhabitants of any decade before us, we believed ourselves in a time of our own making. The dim winter day in 1963 when I first drove up to the La Honda house, truant from my attempts at writing a novel, I knew that the future lay before us and I was certain that we owned it. When Kesey came out, we sat on the little bridge over the creek in the last of the light and smoked what was left of the day's clean weed. Ken said something runic about books never being finished and tales remaining forever untold.[3]

Then, Ron Popeil's Veg-O-Matic made its debut at Chicago's International Housewares Show in 1963, right at the tipping point into "Me." The TV ads that introduced this new appliance to America would also introduce new levels of overstatement and hype:

ME This is Veg-O-Matic, the world famous food-appliance! Slice a whole potato in uniform slices with one motion. Bulk cheese costs less. Look how easy Veg-O-Matic, makes many slices at once! Imagine slicing all these radishes in just seconds. This is the only appliance in the world that slices whole firm tomatoes in one stroke, with every seed in place. Hamburger lovers feed whole onions into Veg-O-Matic, and make these tempting thin slices. Simply turn the dial and change from thin to thick slices. Now, you can slice a whole can of prepared meat at one time. Isn't that amazing? Like magic, dial from slicing to dicing.[4]

The year 1963 was also when Beatlemania swept England like a prairie fire and opened the door for the "British Invasion" of '64 to the remainder of the Western world. Then Dusty Springfield became the second Brit to have a major hit that year. Her first one, "I Only Want to Be with You,"

Library of Congress

rode the charts for the first quarter of '64 before she followed it up with several others. During the next two years Herman's Hermits, the Rolling Stones, Donovan, the Troggs, the Animals, Chad & Jeremy, Peter and Gordon, Petula Clark, Freddie and the Dreamers, Wayne Fontana and the Mind-benders, and Manfred Mann would also have hit singles. And let's not forget the Kinks and the Dave Clark Five. Here are a few of the number-one songs of that period:

Figure 12.4 Music themes from an upswing into "ME."

POPULAR MUSIC THEMES: FIRST HALF OF AN UPSWING INTO "ME" (1963–1973) ME	
	LIFE IS BEAUTIFUL AND ANYTHING IS POSSIBLE
1964: "I Want to Hold Your Hand," The Beatles	MESSAGE
And when I touch you I feel happy inside.	I want to touch you. Right now.
1965: "(I Can't Get No) Satisfaction," The Rolling Stones	
And I'm doin' this and I'm signing that And I'm tryin' to make some girl Who tells me, "Baby, better come back later next week."	Life is all about satisfying your urges.
1966: "Good Vibrations," The Beach Boys	
I'm pickin' up good vibrations. She's giving me excitations.	My girlfriend makes me feel good. She turns me on.
"I Want to Hold Your Hand'" The Beatles	I want to touch you. Right now.
"(I Can't Get No) Satisfaction," The Rolling Stones	Life is all about satisfying your urges.
"A Whiter Shade of Pale," Procol Harum	Eat, drink and be merry, for tomorrow you may die.
"Hey Jude," The Beatles	Don't be down—be happy!
"Imagine," John Lennon	If only . . .
"American Pie," Don McLean	Goodbye, good ol' days.

(CC Image © Wonker on Flickr)

John Steinbeck had hung on to the Upswing of a "We" until it reached its Zenith in 1943 and then rode the Downswing like a little boy sliding down the banister of a stairway. In 1966, three years after the tipping point into "Me," Steinbeck wrote,

 One of the generalities most often noted about Americans is that we are a restless, a dissatisfied, a searching people. We spend our time searching for security, and hate it when we get it. For the most part we are an intemperate people: We eat too much when we can, drink too much, indulge our senses too much. Even in our so-called virtues we are intemperate: a teetotaler is not content not to drink—he must stop all the drinking in the world; a vegetarian among us would outlaw the eating of meat. We work too hard, and many die under the strain; and then to make up for that we play with a violence as suicidal.[5]

By 1967, the fifth year of the six-year transitionary cycle into "Me," the Beatles were no longer singing "I Want to Hold Your Hand," but rather,

ME Crabalocker fishwife, pornographic priestess,
Boy, you been a naughty girl, you let your knickers down.
I am the eggman, they are the eggmen.
I am the walrus! goo goo g'joob.

Mysticism and symbolism shimmer in a "Me," and we are strongly attracted to them. Song lyrics that mean nothing at all suddenly seem deep and mysterious to us. The mysterious predictions of Nostradamus beckon us, and we believe in the magic of pyramids and crystals. We can find profound meaning in virtually anything—"It's all just so meaningful!"

1967: "A Whiter Shade of Pale,"

Procol Harum	MESSAGE
When we called out for another drink,	**Eat, drink and be merry,**
And the waiter brought a tray.	**for tomorrow you may die.**

1968: "Hey Jude," The Beatles

And any time you feel the pain, hey Jude, refrain.	**Don't be down—be happy!**
Don't carry the world upon your shoulders.	

I'm OK, You're OK appeared in 1967, hit the *New York Times* Best-Seller List in 1972, and sold more than fifteen million copies. The title refers to the fourth of four "life positions" that each of us may take:

1. I'm not OK, you're OK.
2. I'm not OK, you're not OK.
3. I'm OK, you're not OK.
4. I'm OK, you're OK.

The message of the book is essentially, "Feel good about yourself, and let other people do their own thing," so it should come as no surprise that the book appeared in the latter part of a six-year transitionary window into "Me." The reason it sold fifteen million copies is because it reinforced a popular opinion.

Interestingly, those same four "life positions" summarize the collective feelings of society's majority at four different positions of the Pendulum.

1. I'm not OK, you're OK:

In the second half of the Upswing into "Me" and in the first half of the Downswing from it (1973–1993) hero worship and a struggle against self-doubt define us. Envy and anxiousness cause us to overcompensate, leading to costumes, posing, and big hair.

2. I'm not OK, you're not OK:

The second half of the Downswing of "Me" and the first half of an Upswing into "We" bring us self-doubt and a general awareness of brokenness (1993–2013). This often becomes a cause for communion and fellowship, as broken persons are transparent to one another. Interestingly, during the six-year transitionary window into "We" the mutual brokenness of "I'm not OK, you're not OK" often translates into a feeling of mutual acceptance: "I'm OK, you're OK." The last time this happened was when Gen-X passed the torch to Gen-Y during the 2003–2008 transitionary window.

3. I'm OK, you're not OK:

The second half of the Upswing of "We" and the first half of the Downswing from it (2013–2023) bring an ideological "righteousness" that seems to spring from any group gathered around a cause. The inevitable result is judgmental legalism and witch hunts. The origin of the term *witch hunt* was the Salem witch trials, a series of hearings before county court officials to prosecute people accused of witchcraft in the counties of Essex, Suffolk, and Middlesex in colonial Massachusetts, between February 1692 and May 1693,[6] exactly at the beginning of the second half of the Upswing toward the "We" Zenith of 1703.

Senator Joseph McCarthy was an American promoter of this witch-hunt attitude at America's most recent "We" Zenith of 1943 (see the "House Un-American Activities Committee," 1937–1953); Adolph Hitler was the German promoter (see the Holocaust, 1933–1945); and Joseph Stalin was the Soviet promoter (see the Great Purge, 1936–1938). Our hope is that we might collectively choose to skip this development as we approach the "We" Zenith of 2023. If enough of us are aware of this trend toward judgmental self-righteousness, perhaps we can resist demonizing those who disagree with us and avoid the societal polarization that results from it. A truly great society is one in which being unpopular can be safe.

4. I'm OK, you're OK:

The second half of the Downswing from "We" brings us the happy message of the Alpha Voices, "Hey, everybody! We're *ALL* okay!" and the resulting glow of confidence that follows during the first half of the Upswing into "Me" as we elevate sparkling cultural heroes we admire. During the second half of the Upswing into "Me" is when envy and self-doubt begin to plague us, and then everything becomes a competition as we move back into "I'm not OK, you're OK"—and the cycle begins anew.

The six years of magic we remember as "the '60s" began in 1963 and continued through the end of 1968. Just as 1960 to 1962 weren't part of "the '60s," 1969 wasn't part of that magic either. Look in the rearview mirror and you'll see that 1969 was the first year of the '70s, the seventh year of an Upswing, when the most sensitive among us began to notice that we were taking a good thing too far. What began as a beautiful dream of individuality and freedom of expression was devolving into plastic, hollow, phony posing.

In 1971, Hunter S. Thompson remembered the Democratic National Convention held in Chicago in late August of 1968:

ME There was no point in fighting—on our side or theirs. We had all the momentum; we were riding the crest of a high and beautiful wave . . . So now, less than five years later, you can go up on a steep hill in Las Vegas and look West, and with the right kind of eyes you can almost see the high-water mark—the place where the wave finally broke and rolled back.[7]

I still have trouble when I think about Chicago. That week at the Convention changed everything I'd ever taken for granted about this country and my place in it. . . . Every time I tried to tell somebody what happened in Chicago I began crying, and it took me years to understand why . . . Chicago was the End of the Sixties, for me.[8]

He also wrote that

ME The hippies, who had never really believed they were the wave of the future anyway, saw the election results as brutal confirmation of the futility of fighting the establishment on its own terms. The thrust is no longer for 'change' or 'progress' or 'revolution,' but merely to escape, to live on the far perimeter of a world that might have been.[9]

The six-year transitionary window is always a beautiful time of change for the better. But for the perceptive person, the seventh year gives pause as he or she sees the momentum of society carrying a good thing too far. These people, like Hunter S. Thompson before them, see the once-bright dream of a better world begin to yellow and crumble at the edges like an old poster on a bedroom wall.

The year 1971 was also when John Lennon wrote what is perhaps the definitive song of that era. "Imagine" speaks dreamily of what could be—"if only." In 2004, *Rolling Stone* ranked "Imagine" as number three in the *500 Greatest Songs of All Time*. (The song rated number one was "Like a Rolling Stone" by Bob Dylan and number two was "Satisfaction" by the Rolling Stones. If we discount their top two choices due to the magazine's obvious self-interest, John Lennon's "Imagine" suddenly becomes the number-one song of the forty-year "Me":

ME You may say I'm a dreamer
But I'm not the only one.
I hope someday you'll join us
And the world will live as one.

Remember: A "Me" is about big dreams; a "We" is about small actions. The glowing dream of John Lennon's "Imagine" began to shimmer and fade at the end of the six-year transitionary window.

Hunter S. Thompson could feel that the purity of our dreams had somehow slipped through our fingers. Everyone could feel it, apparently, because all of Western society indulged in a moment of nostalgic reflection in 1971 before plunging headlong toward 1983, the pinnacle of "Me."

Mix individuality with freedom of expression, and the result will always be symbolic and mystical. The perfect example of this is the top song of 1972, right at the halfway point of "Me":

1972: "American Pie," Don McLean

In the lyrics of this song Don McLean recalled the music of the Alpha Voices from when he was a boy in the late 1950s. He sung symbolically of Buddy Holly's death in a plane crash on February 3, 1959, and how Buddy's pregnant wife, now a widow after barely six months of marriage, miscarried the baby soon after the plane crash. McLean then made a backhanded reference to "The Book of Love," a hit song by the Monotones at the time of the crash. He sung of Bob Dylan, "the jester," who sang "in a coat he borrowed from James Dean," referring to the jacket Dylan wore on the cover of his album *Freewheelin'*, which made him look very much like James Dean in *Rebel without a Cause*. McLean then sung of "the jester," Bob Dylan, stealing the crown of "the king," Elvis Presley, while Elvis was in the Army.

McLean then sung cryptically about how the Warren Commission failed to resolve the Kennedy assassination due to Jack Ruby's murder of Lee Harvey Oswald: "No verdict was returned."

The song then moved on to speak of Lennon reading a book of Marx while "the quartet practiced in the park."

For those familiar with the lyrics of the song, "Helter Skelter" is a song written by Paul McCartney and recorded by the Beatles in 1968.

Rehab facilities were sometimes called "fallout shelters." The Byrds recorded "Eight Miles High" in 1966. "Sergeant Pepper's Lonely Hearts Club Band" was a 1967 album by the Beatles.

"Jack Flash sat on a candlestick" referred to *Jumpin' Jack Flash*, a hit by the Rolling Stones in 1968.

"No angel born in hell" referred to the Hells Angels motorcycle gang, which functioned as security for the Rolling Stones. In Altamont, California, on December 6, 1969, Alan Passaro, one of the Hell's Angels, stabbed to death an eighteen-year-old girl, Meredith Hunter, who was armed with a revolver and trying to climb on stage.

The "girl who sang the blues" is likely Janis Joplin, a rock-and-roll blues singer who had just died of an overdose in 1970. *Rolling Stone* ranked Janis Joplin as number twenty-eight on its 2008 list of 100 Greatest Singers of All Time. Her death was recent news when McLean wrote *American Pie*.

According to McLean,

ME *American Pie* really was . . . an idea in my head after I thought about the death of Buddy Holly . . . and that whole period of my life when I was a teenager . . . and from that, I developed an idea which I was going to turn into a parable . . . a story with a moral . . . which originally had nothing to do with Bob Dylan, The Beatles, or The Stones . . . It was a story about America. And the fact that people were drawn into the song as a result of symbols that I chose to use, was the reason I chose to use those symbols in the first place.[10]

Further, if Asia is indeed headed into a "Me" while the Americas, Australia, and western Europe are headed into a "We," right now

China should have its own Jack Kerouac/Holden Caulfield/James Dean "Rebel without a Cause" antiestablishment hero, correct?

Meet Han Han, the Chinese James Dean. Just as Kerouac, Caulfield, and Dean embodied the Alpha Voice teen angst seven years before our 1963 tipping point into "Me," Han Han embodied the teen angst of China when he published his first novel, *Triple Door*, and dropped out of the tenth grade in 1999, just four years before China reached the "Me" tipping point of 2003.

Han Han has since become the preeminent voice inspiring youthful rebellion and the rejection of traditional values in China. Evan Osnos, writing for the July 4, 2011 *New Yorker*, called Han Han's first book "a scathingly realistic satire of education and authority, written by a nobody."

The first edition of thirty thousand copies of Han Han's *Triple Door* sold out in just three days. The second edition of thirty thousand sold out even faster. When China Central Television tried to calm the frenzy with an hour-long interrogation of Han Han on its national broadcast, the insolent and defiant Han Han became China's national symbol of individuality and freedom of expression. His novels about teenagers, girls, and cars continue to sell millions of copies to the *baling hou,* the "post '80s generation" of China who came of age as that nation was approaching 2003, the tipping point into the current Eastern "Me." According to Osnos, "the *baling hou* serve as a reference point in discussions of values and the national character much the way that baby boomers do for Americans."

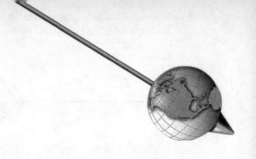

Pendulum Legend

At its Zenith, the message of "Me" is conspicuous
consumption. Get all you can.

CHAPTER THIRTEEN

1973–1983:
The Upswing of "Me"
Reaches Its Limit

The second half of an Upswing of "Me" is when the new values adopted during the six-year transitionary window have so fully permeated our society that we become largely unaware of their influence. The happy, bouncy purity of "being true to yourself" has begun to degenerate into a contest over who is the most unique.

When we're not being symbolic and cryptic in a "Me," we're singing sappy-happy songs and jingles about "apple trees and honey bees and snow-white turtledoves." Do you remember *Jonathan Livingston Seagull?*

The following are the best-selling books of 1973 according to *Publishers Weekly.*

Figure 13.1 *Best-selling books from an upswing into "ME."*

BEST-SELLING BOOKS IN AN UPSWING OF "ME" (1973)	ME

1. *Jonathan Livingston Seagull,* Richard Bach

This is the parable of a seagull that breaks away from the flock and sets out to find himself. More than a million of us read it and said dreamily, "I see myself in that bird . . . He flies so high. . . all alone. . . and no one understands him. Yes, that bird is me.

2. *Once Is Not Enough,* Jacqueline Susann

This is the story of a young woman's drug use and sexual escapades. The book ends as she tries LSD and takes part in an orgy. She then wanders onto the beach, where she hallucinates that she sees her father and walks into the ocean after him, presumably drowning.

3. *Breakfast of Champions,* Kurt Vonnegut

The story of "two lonesome, skinny, fairly old white men on a planet which was dying fast." One of these men, Dwayne Hoover, is a normal-looking but deeply deranged Pontiac dealer and Burger Chef franchise owner who becomes obsessed with the writings of a science fiction author, Kilgore Trout, taking them for literal truth. Dwayne Hoover comes to believe that he, Dwayne Hoover, is the only individual in the universe with free will.[1]

These are the international hit songs of 1973.

Figure 13.2   Popular music themes during a "ME" Zenith.

POPULAR MUSIC THEMES: AN UPSWING OF "ME" REACHES ITS LIMITS I (1973) ME

SYMBOLIC AND CRYPTIC AND SINGING SAPPY-HAPPY SONGS

	MESSAGE
1. **"Angie,"** The Rolling Stones	
Angie, you're beautiful, but ain't it time we said good-bye?	**I loved you. I had you. Now I'm leaving you.**
2. **"Tie a Yellow Ribbon Round the Ole Oak Tree,"** Tony Orlando & Dawn	
Now the whole damn bus is cheering And I can't believe I see A hundred yellow ribbons 'round the old oak tree. I'm comin' home.	**I needed forgiveness and you gave it to me. Life is good!**
3. **"Killing Me Softly with His Song,"** Roberta Flack	
He sang as if he knew me in all my dark despair and then he looked right through me as if I wasn't there.	**I was in pain but a song made me feel better.**
4. **"You're So Vain,"** Carly Simon	
You're so vain, I'll bet you think this song is about you. Don't you? Don't you? Don't you?	**Even though you're successful, you're still posing.**

ME What began as a beautiful dream of individuality and freedom of expression was devolving into plastic, hollow, phony posing.
—*Michael R. Drew*

Carly Simon's "You're So Vain" reminds me of a comment one of our board members made to a classroom full of business owners assembled at Wizard Academy on July 1, 2007. Dr. Richard D. Grant, a renowned psychologist and a teacher of consumer behavior in the MBA program at the University of Texas, said,

ME The great problem in the United States is not repression or neurosis, which it was in Europe when Freud wrote about everything. No, the great problem here is not repression—it's narcissism and addiction. Those are our great problems in the United States because Tommy Jefferson set us up. "Life, Liberty, and the . . . *Pursuit of Happiness!*" If you pursue happiness directly, it evades you. *But you feel entitled to it* . . . It's wonderful, but it has a dark side. And the dark side is addiction. Addiction. We have done a dance with addiction in this country from the very beginning.

Freud wrote about repression during the Upswing of a "We." His core belief was, "If it feels good, do it." Freud believed self-denial to be the root of virtually every psychological problem. Freud was a champion of "Me."

5. "The Ballroom Blitz," The Sweet	MESSAGE
And the man in the back said 'Everyone attack,' And it turned into a ballroom blitz.	**It's fun when things get crazy and out of control.**

6. "Crocodile Rock," Elton John	
Well, Crocodile Rocking is something shocking when your feet just can't keep still. I never knew me a better time and I guess I never will."	**I remember the innocence and simplicity of yesterday.**

In 1978, a decade since 1968, the final year of our six-year transitionary window, we were only five years out from the Zenith of "Me."

During this time rock and roll took a lesson from Las Vegas and leapt into over-the-top showmanship. Put a cowboy, a policeman, a construction worker, an Indian chief, a biker and a G.I. on stage in full costume and what have you got? The Village People:

 It's fun to stay at the Y-M-C-A!
They have everything that you need to enjoy.
You can hang out with all the boys . . .
It's fun to stay at the Y-M-C-A!

Watching the Village People was as if society had said, "Now that we've discovered the spectacle of circuses, let's see how far we can push it."

Do you remember the studded, black leather outfits and grease-paint makeup of the rock band KISS? Groups like these soared during the second half of the Upswing of "Me," as our hunger for individuality entered the realm of costumes.

Yes, things were getting out of hand.

Today we look back on bands like KISS and the Village People and realize how silly they were. But that wasn't our feeling at the time. Looking proudly at us from the posters on our walls, these bands said, "These aren't costumes—we're just expressing the real person that each of us is inside. Each member of this band is unique and special and different. And don't you wish you were me?"

Strangely, KISS and the Village People weren't the Zenith of the "Me"; they were merely two of the strange bands leading up to it.

1983: Zenith of "Me"

When we finally get to the Zenith of "Me," we find there's nothing there. Individuality has degenerated into a costume party. Men no longer walk on the beach; they just move forward by striking a series of poses. The once-heartfelt music of singer-songwriters has devolved into big hair, disco, and glam rock. In business, "branding campaigns" are when advertisers wear costumes to the Media Masquerade Ball.

Figure 13.3 Moving into a Zenith of "ME."

Marketers are paid to make promises that businesses have no intention of keeping.

Literature in a "Me" thrives on fantasy, terror, and heroes. Take a look at the best-selling books for 1983 according to *Publishers Weekly*.

Figure 13.4 Popular Literature in the Zenith of a "ME" cycle."

POPULAR LITERATURE THEMES: ZENITH OF A "ME" CYCLE (1983) ME

1. *Return of the Jedi*, James Kahn

Written as a companion to the blockbuster movie, the book describes how the savior of the universe, Luke Skywalker, rescues his friend, Han Solo, from the vile gangster, Jabba the Hutt. Meanwhile, Darth Vader makes plans to crush the Rebel Alliance once and for all.

2. *Poland*, James Michener

This is a saga about generations of people in Bukowo, Poland, where, "A Pole is a man born with a sword in his right hand, a brick in his left. When the battle is over, he starts to rebuild."

3. *Pet Cemetery*, Stephen King

This is a horror story about an ancient burial ground of the Micmac Indians that brings the dead back to life.

That year, slick, tight, polished, professional, and fully choreographed, Michael Jackson swept the American Grammys with an unprecedented eight wins in this pinnacle year of his career. The music videos of his album *Thriller* featured zombies, ghouls, werewolves, and mummies as rock stars. It became the best-selling album of all time, with the sales of over 110 million copies worldwide.

Here's a quick look at the compiled, international list of Hit Songs for all of Western society that year. Individuality and *sensation* are the heart and soul of the Zenith of "Me."

Figure 13.5 Popular Literature in the Zenith of a "ME" cycle."

POPULAR MUSIC THEMES: ZENITH OF A "ME" CYCLE (1983)	ME

1. "Flashdance . . . What a Feeling,"
Irene Cara

MESSAGE

Take your passion,
and make it happen.
Pictures come alive,
you can dance right through your life."

I can do anything.

2. "Billie Jean," Michael Jackson

Billie Jean is not my lover.
She's just a girl who claims that I am the one.
But the kid is not my son.

I refuse to take responsibility for the child I fathered.

3. "Every Breath You Take," The Police

How my poor heart aches
with every step you take, every move you make,
every vow you break, every smile you fake,
every claim you stake.
I'll be watching you.

I am obsessed with you and I must have you.

4. "Karma Chameleon," Culture Club

I'm a man without conviction. I'm a man who doesn't know how to sell a contradiction.

CC Image courtesy of Andrew Hurley on Flickr

Although there's been much speculation, no one has ever been entirely sure what this song is about. The writer of the song, Boy George, was a heroin addict who later went to prison for assault and the false imprisonment of a male escort. Remember, mystical symbolism, extreme sensation, and individuality tend to spiral out of control at the Zenith of a "Me."

5. **"99 Red Balloons,"** Nena	MESSAGE
Panic bells, it's red alert. There's something here from somewhere else. The war machine springs to life.	**Everyone is poised to overreact— a bag of balloons could start a war.**

6. **"Let's Dance,"** David Bowie	
Let's sway while color lights up your face Let's sway through the crowd to an empty space.	**Let's dance and sway and live this moment together. Right now.**

And guess who made her debut in 1983, right at the Zenith of "Me?"

Madonna, of course.

And what was her big breakout song?

CC Image courtesy of iShot71 on Flickr

ME 'Cause we are living in a material world, and I am a material girl!

When individuality is taken to its logical conclusion, each of us feels we have to be more individual than anyone else. It becomes a contest.

At its Zenith, the message of "Me" is conspicuous consumption: "Get all you can. Can all you get. Sit on the can. Poison the rest. Whoever dies with the most toys wins. Second place is the first loser. Winning is all that matters. Poverty sucks."

At the Zenith of the previous "Me" (1903), Teddy Roosevelt armed himself with the Sherman Antitrust Act to fight the robber barons of his day. Rapacious greed is applauded as "good business" near the Zenith of a "Me." A new breed of robber barons made their appearance eighty years later, just as we approached the Zenith of 1983. Carl Icahn, T. Boone Pickens, Ivan Boesky, Kirk Kerkorian, and Michael

T. Boone Pickens

Milken are just five of the thirty-two robber barons of that era you'll find listed under "Corporate Raiders" on Wikipedia.

And who were our movie heroes in the forty-year "Me" of 1963 to 2003?

- Sean Connery—*James Bond* (1962–1971): "Bond. James Bond."

- Clint Eastwood—*Dirty Harry, Sudden Impact* (1971, 1983): "Go ahead. Make my day."

- Bruce Willis—*Die Hard* (1–3, 1988–1995): "Yippee-ki-yay, motherfucker."

- Keanu Reeves—*The Matrix* (1999–2003): "Morpheus believes he [Neo] is The One."

But the heroes in a "Me" aren't always greedy and self-serving like the robber barons or violent and defiant like the myths of the silver screen—there are also some excellent role models to be found.

Pendulum Legend

Propelled by the momentum of the society around
them, leaders at the Zenith of a "Me" tend to
become very full of themselves.

CHAPTER FOURTEEN

Three Thousand Years of "Me": A "Me" Is About Big Dreams

iStockphoto / Vii-Studio

These are the representative voices that capture the spirits of every "Me" for the past three thousand years. Keep in mind that the twenty-year Upswing into a "Me" Zenith occurs only once every eighty years. You'll notice that some "Me" Upswings are represented by an event that embodied the times, whereas others are marked by an individual life. If that chosen person enjoyed a lifespan that touched both sides of the Pendulum, the Zenith in question will be the one at which that person made their mark on the world.

Figure 14.1 Values and beliefs in society during a "ME" cycle.

"ME" IS ABOUT . . .	ME

1. Freedom of expression
2. Personal liberty
3. One man is wiser than a million men.
4. Wants to achieve a better life—"I came, I saw, I *conquered.*"
5. Big dreams
6. Wants to be number one
7. Individual confidence and decisive persons
8. Leadership is "Look at me. Admire me. Emulate me if you can."
9. Elevates attractive heroes to strengthen society's sense of identity

iStockphoto / mmac72

Not all the Zenith-beats are equally loud, but the rhythm of society's heart remains constant just the same. We'll begin as we did in the previous list with Solomon, who experienced both sides of the Pendulum in his lifespan of eighty years.

Figure 14.2 Values of "ME" Zenith when society takes a good thing too far.

ZENITHS OF "ME" OVER THE LAST THREE THOUSAND YEARS	ME

977 BCE: *Solomon is King.* And young (about thirty-four years old). And at the Zenith of a "Me."

I said to myself, "Come now, I will test you with pleasure to find out what is good" . . . I tried cheering myself with wine, and embracing folly . . . I undertook great projects: I built houses for myself and planted vineyards. I made gardens and parks and planted all kinds of fruit trees in them. I made reservoirs to water groves of flourishing trees. I bought male and female slaves and had other slaves who were born in my house. I also owned more herds and flocks than anyone in Jerusalem before me. I amassed silver and gold for myself, and the treasure of kings and provinces. I acquired male and female singers, and a harem as well—the delights of a man's heart. I became greater by far than anyone in Jerusalem before me.

I denied myself nothing my eyes desired; I refused my heart no pleasure.

897 BCE: *King Ahab of Israel and Jezebel,* his wife, desired the vineyard of Naboth, their neighbor. He refused to sell, so they had him killed. This is a very famous "Me" episode in the Bible (1 Kings 21). The *Encyclopedia Americana* lists this event as happening in 897 BCE, but many scholars list it a few years past this Zenith of "Me."

The ends justify the means.

817 BCE: *Jehu "drives like a maniac."* Joram, son of Ahab, is King of Israel. When Jehu decided to kill Joram, he thundered off in his chariot like a hero in an action film.

When the lookout standing on the tower in Jezreel saw Jehu's troops approaching, he called out, "I see some troops coming."

"Get a horseman," Joram ordered. "Send him to meet them and ask, 'Do you come in peace?'"

The horseman rode off to meet Jehu and said, "This is what the king says: 'Do you come in peace?'"

"What do you have to do with peace?" Jehu replied. "Fall in behind me."

The lookout reported, "The messenger has reached them, but he isn't coming back."

So the king sent out a second horseman. When he came to them he said, "This is what the king says: 'Do you come in peace?'"

Jehu replied, "What do you have to do with peace? Fall in behind me."

The lookout reported, "He has reached them, but he isn't coming back either. The driving is like that of Jehu son of Nimshi—he drives like a maniac."

—*2 Kings 9*

Jehu shot Joram through the heart with an arrow. As he was leaving, Joram's mother, Jezebel, shouts something insolent at Jehu from the window of a tower.

He looked up at the window and called out, "Who is on my side? Who?" Two or three eunuchs looked down at him. "Throw her down!" Jehu said. So they threw her down, and some of her blood spattered the wall and the horses as they trampled her underfoot.

—*2 Kings 9*

Other men walk, but I explode onto the scene. I am Jehu.

737 BCE: *Isaiah* became a prophet in Israel on the Upswing of this "Me" (about 742 BCE) and served as a guiding light in that nation for more than sixty years.

Dynamic figures often emerge during a "Me." Some of these are infamously bad, like Ahab and Jezebel, whereas others are heroic and good, like Isaiah.

Here am I; send me!

---

667 BCE: *King Byzas* of Megara (near Athens) founded Byzantium after asking the Oracle at Delphi where he should build his city. She told him to build it "opposite the blind." Byzas had no idea what she meant, but when he sailed the Bosporus he suddenly understood: on the eastern shore was a Greek city, Chalcedon, whose founders had overlooked a superior location only 1.9 miles away. Byzas founded his city "opposite" Chalcedon on the western shore and named it Byzantium, after himself.[1] The city was later renamed Constantinople and was, for a time, the imperial residence of Emperor Constantine. Then it was the capital of the Byzantine Empire (the Greek-speaking Roman Empire of late Antiquity and the Middle Ages) for more than a thousand years. Byzantium/Constantinople became Istanbul in 1930.

My dream and my destiny are to build a royal city.

---

577 BCE: *The Circus Maximus in Rome* (575 BCE) opened late during the rule of Tarquinius Priscus. The Circus Maximus was a legendary chariot-racing track, Rome's original spectacle. According to *Ab Urbe Condita Libri*, or *Chapters from the Foundation of the City*, by the Roman historian Titus Livius (59 BCE–CE 17), horses and boxers from Etruria were the first to participate in the annual games that began at this time. The city was then known as Rumula (named after Romulus), but was the name later shortened to Rome.

A city? You say you're going to build a city? I'll show you a city.

---

497 BCE: *Aulus Postumius Albus Regillensis* led an infant Rome to victory over the Latin League at the Battle of Lake Regillus (496 BCE). This is the beginning of the Roman legend of Castor and Pollux, the twins of the constellation Gemini, who, according to legend, assisted the Romans in the battle. Because one twin was mortal and the other immortal, Castor and Pollux became symbols of the idea that death and immortality are not opposites but rather twinned, thus leading to the definitive "Me" statement of every conqueror, every warrior.

To die with valor is to become immortal.

417 BCE: *Socrates,* now fifty-two years old and in his prime, openly objected to the democratic government of Athens. Plato, his star pupil, would later say that the only good government would be the rule of a Philosopher-King.

One man is wiser than a million men.

337 BCE: *Alexander the Great* assumed the throne of Macedonia (336 BCE) upon the murder of his father and quickly began his conquest of the world. When Alexander died in his early thirties, he left no strong government behind, so his largely unprotected empire became easy pickings for the ambitious leaders of Rome, a young city-state on the move.

The world needs a king—me.

257 BC: *The tribes of Rome* reached their pinnacle of thirty-five during the Upswing of this "Me," with each Tribe having its own tribunal to represent them in all civil, religious, and military affairs. Rome originally comprised just three tribes: the Ramnes, Tities, and Luceres. But during a "Me" groups tend to splinter as opposed to coming together as they do in a "We."

To hell with working together; I'm making sure my family comes out on top.

177 BCE: *The Circus Maximus* was rebuilt in marble three stories high (it was previously wooden) and spectacular gates are added. This ancient Roman chariot racing stadium was now 2,037 feet in length and 387 feet in width and could accommodate about 150,000 spectators. It shouted to the world,

Behold! And be amazed at the magnificence that is Rome.

97 BCE: *Hillel the Elder*—one of the most important figures in Jewish history, is associated with developing both the Mishnah and the Talmud, and is renowned within Judaism as a sage and scholar—has his Bar Mitzvah and soon began to make his mark on the world. Hillel understood the healthy aspects of "Me" and has been remembered for it for more than two thousand years. Two of his most famous sayings are:

If not now, when? and If I am not for myself, who will be for me? And when I am for myself, what am "I"?

17 BCE: *Caesar Augustus,* previously known as Octavius, became the first emperor of Rome in 27 BCE, when the Pendulum was halfway to this Zenith. At the age of twenty-five, Tiberius was made "pontifex maximus," the high priest of the religion of ancient Rome, just two years prior to the Zenith. He would be the second emperor of Rome thirty-one years later. According to Tacitus, Tiberius derided the Roman Senate as "men fit to be slaves."

I am better than the best.

63 CE: *Nero,* perhaps the definitive, out-of-control "Me," was then in full swing as emperor of Rome, having begun his reign in the middle of the Upswing of the "Me" in 54 CE. His reign is associated with tyranny, debauchery, and excess. Many believe Nero started the great fire of Rome in 64 CE in order to obtain just a small part of the land that he wanted. According to the writings of Tacitus, Suetonius, and Cassius Dio, Nero was also known for having Christians burned in his garden at night for a source of light. Facing certain assassination, he committed suicide on June 9, 68 CE. Sounds a little like Adolph Hitler, doesn't he?

You want to see crazy? I'll show you crazy.

143 CE: *No Strong "Me"* leader emerges at this time. The current Roman emperor, Antoninus Pius, just two years prior to this "Me" Zenith, instituted the Puellae Faustinianae, a charitable foundation for daughters of the poorer people of Rome.

What!? A "We" leader at the Zenith of a "Me"? This will lead to disastrous consequences forty years later, at the Zenith of the "We" in 183.

You haven't forgotten about Nero, have you?

223 CE: *Emperor Elagabalus,* just three years prior to the Zenith, announced that the Syrian sun god, El-Gabal, for whom he is priest, was the only true god. Soon thereafter his own Praetorian Guard murdered Elagabalus while he was in a latrine.

I am the spokesman for God.

303 CE: *Emperor Galerius* miraculously turned the tide of the war against Persia and defeated the king, Narseh, just six years prior to this Zenith. He then reconquered Mesopotamia. Full of "Me" at the Zenith, on February 24, 303, Galerius insisted that edicts of persecution be issued against the Christians. Galerius maintained this policy of repression until he issued a general edict of toleration in April 311, apparently during his last bout of illness, shortly before he died from a horribly gruesome disease Eusebius later described, possibly some form of bowel cancer, gangrenem or Fournier gangrene.[2]

Woe to him that I do not favor, for I have the power to hurt.

383 CE: *Emperor Theodosius the Great,* perhaps suspicious of what happened to emperors Galerius and Elagabalus, declared Christianity to be the official religion of the Roman Empire. Propelled by the momentum of the society around them, leaders at the Zenith of a "Me" tend to become very full of themselves.

You must believe as I believe.

463 CE: *Attila* became king of the Huns just before a "Me" and consolidated his power throughout the Upswing of that "Me" to its Zenith. Callinicus, in his *Life of Saint Hypatius,* wrote,

> The barbarian nation of the Huns, which was in Thrace, became so great that more than a hundred cities were captured and Constantinople almost came into danger and most men fled from it. . . . And there were so many murders and blood-lettings that the dead could not be numbered. Ay, for they took captive the churches and monasteries and slew the monks and maidens in great numbers.

Make no mistake—I'm bad to the bone.

543 CE: *Belisarius* was the hero of Rome. During the Upswing of this "Me" this Roman general defeated the army of Xerxes, defeated the Vandals at Ad Decimum, captured the city of Carthage, and so thoroughly reconquered North Africa that the Vandals ceased to exist as a unified tribe. Then he captured the city of Ravenna. When the Bulgars were invading Constantinople in 558, who did Justinian the Great call out of retirement to repel them? Belisarius, of course. In 565 Belisarius died in a peaceful retirement at the age of sixty. Now *that's* a hero.

If I had tights and a cape, I believe I could fly.

623 CE: *Muhammad,* the founder of Islam, was fifty-three years old and halfway finished transcribing the Quran at the Zenith of this "Me." Muslims believe that the Quran was verbally revealed to Muhammad through the angel Jibril (Gabriel) over a period of twenty-three years beginning in 610 CE, when Muhammad was forty, and concluding in 632 CE, the year of his death.[3] Muhammad is a classic hero, easy to admire and active as a diplomat, merchant, philosopher, orator, legislator, reformer, and military general. In 1718 Simon Ockley wrote in his book, *The History of the Saracen Empires,* "The greatest success of Mohammad's life was effected by sheer moral force."

To the light I have attained and in the light I live.

703 CE: *Archdeacon Paschal* tried to buy the Papacy, and archpriest Theodore tried to steal it during the Upswing of this "Me." (These things just don't happen during a "We.") The mass of clergy, however, set Paschal and Theodore both aside and chose Sergius, who was duly consecrated. To his credit, Sergius (later to become Pope St. Sergius I) attempted to recruit the Venerable Bede as his adviser.

The wicked struggle for power, and the good protect it from them.

783 CE: *Byzantine Emperor Constantine VI* was in the third year of his reign. He was twelve years old and had been engaged for a year to Rotrude, a daughter of Charlemagne. When he was twenty-one, Kardam of Bulgaria defeated him in battle, and Constantine VI did not respond with enough style and glamour to satisfy his followers, so a movement developed to elevate his uncle Caesar Nikephoros to become the empire's new emperor.

Constantine responded by having his uncle's eyes put out and cutting off the tongues of his father's four other half-brothers. He then divorced his wife because she had failed to provide him with a male heir and married his mistress. The people needed a hero, and Constantine VI obviously wasn't it, so at the age of twenty-six he was apprehended and cruelly blinded by his captors, dying of his wounds a few days later.

Be an elegant captain when society is in a "Me" or your people will throw you overboard.

863 CE: *Al-Battani* solved the riddles of the sun and the stars in 877 AD. His calculations would be instrumental in helping Tycho Brahe, Kepler, Galileo, and Copernicus solve their own riddles six hundred years later and two thousand miles away. He wrote,

> After having lengthily applied myself in the study of this science, I have noticed that the works on the movements of the planets differed consistently with each other, and that many authors made errors in the manner of undertaking their observation, and establishing their rules. I also noticed that with time, the position of the planets changed according to recent and older observations; changes caused by the obliquity of the ecliptic, affecting the calculation of the years and that of eclipses. Continuous focus on these things drove me to perfect and confirm such a science.[4]

I did it because it was my passion.

943 CE: *Otto the Great* took the throne of Germany (then known as East Francia) in 936 and arranged for his coronation to be held in Charlemagne's former capital of Aachen. He is duke of Saxony, king of Germany, and king of Italy, ruling all of what will later be called the Holy Roman Empire. Otto dominated the Church and used its unifying power in the German lands to strengthen his grasp on the people. In addition, Otto arranged for close family members to hold all the important duchies.

Might makes right. God is obviously on the side of whoever is winning.

1023 CE: *The Golden Age of Islam* culminated in Persia at this time with the writings of Ibn Sīnā (Avicenna), a polymath and a leader in the development of modern medicine. As a boy, Avicenna is said to have read the *Metaphysics* of Aristotle until the words were imprinted on his memory. He turned to medicine at sixteen and soon discovered new treatments. At eighteen Avicenna wrote, "Medicine is no hard and thorny science, like mathematics and metaphysics, so I soon made great progress; I became an excellent doctor and began to treat patients, using approved remedies." His book, *The Canon of Medicine,* documents his use of experimental medicine, evidence-based medicine, randomized controlled trials, and efficacy tests. It laid out the rules and principles for testing the effectiveness of new drugs and formed the basis of clinical pharmacology and modern clinical trials. Avicenna's principles include:

1. *The drug must be free from any extraneous accidental quality.*

2. *It must be used on a simple, not a composite, disease.*

3. *The drug must be tested with two contrary types of diseases, because sometimes a drug cures one disease by its essential qualities and another by its accidental ones.*

4. *The time of action must be observed, so that essence and accident are not confused.*

5. *The effect of the drug must be seen to occur constantly or in many cases. If this did not happen, it was an accidental effect.*

6. *The experiment must be done with a human, because testing a drug on a lion or a horse might not prove anything about its effect on man.*

When his friends suggested he slow down for the sake of his health, Avicenna said,

I prefer a short life with width to a narrow one with length.

1103 CE: *Pope Urban II* set up the modern-day Roman Curia in the manner of a royal court to help run the Catholic Church. Then he launched the Crusades in 1096, more than halfway up this "Me," thereby triggering a thousand years of conflict between East and West.

I will reconquer Jerusalem.

King Henry I, during the Upswing of this "Me," threw a challenger named Conan Pilatus from the window of a tower of Rouen, which then became known as "Conan's Leap." The men on the ground below tied Conan's lifeless body to a horse's tail and had him dragged through the streets of the city as a warning to other traitors. Henry is famed for holding the record for more than twenty acknowledged illegitimate children, the largest number born to any English king.[5]

If you can't be with the one you love, love the one you're with.

1183 CE: *Richard the Lionheart* would take the throne of England in six short years, but he was already known as "The Lionheart" due to his reputation as a great military leader and warrior. He is one of very few kings of England remembered by his nickname rather than his regnal number (Richard I). Like most "Me" leaders, Richard was less of an administrator than a conqueror. He spent very little time in England, preferring adventure instead. Returning from the Crusades in 1192, his ship was wrecked near Aquileia, forcing Richard and his four companions to take the dangerous land route through central Europe. Although disguised as a Knight Templar, Richard was recognized, and Duke Leopold imprisoned him and then turned him over to Henry VI, King of Germany and Holy Roman Emperor. Richard famously refused to give deference to Henry, saying instead,

I am born of a rank that recognizes no superior but God.

1263 CE: *Shajarat-al-Dur*, a heroic woman, began the Mamluk Dynasty of Egypt in 1250 during the Upswing of this "Me." Further, according to Historian John Fines, at its Zenith in 1263, *Thomas Aquinas*, a thirty-eight-year-old instructor, rocked the world with "teaching that was brilliant and novel, and formed the foundation for his writing. His aim was to introduce his pupils to the 'wonderfulness' of each topic; he held at least three disputations a week, often of the new kind of his own invention, where students flung in questions."[6]

One of the things that made him "Saint" Thomas Aquinas was that he always allowed the other individual to make a full statement of their position.

ME
It is requisite for the relaxation of the mind that we make use, from time to time, of playful deeds and jokes.
—*Thomas Aquinas*

CC Image

1343 CE: *King Edward III* of England claimed the throne of France. The naval fleets of England and France met in the Battle of Sluys, ending with the almost total destruction of the French fleet.

Uh-oh.

1423 CE: *Robin Hood*, that great hero of individualism and rebellion against authority, was made famous in the *Orygynale Chronicle*, written by Andrew of Wyntoun in about 1420.

ME
Lytil Jhon and Robyne HudeWayth-men ware commendyd gude In Yngil-wode and Barnysdale Thai oysyd all this tyme thare trawale.
—*Andrew of Wyntoun*

Andrew of Wyntoun claimed the events of his tale happened in 1283, but in truth he probably fictionalized the whole thing, much like Geoffrey of Monmouth crafted King Arthur and the Knights of the Round Table from the fabric of fertile imagination.

I rob from the rich and give to the poor. I'm a criminal, but you love me anyway.

1503 CE: *Pope Julius II* took the seat of Rome. Nicknamed "The Fearsome Pope" (Il Papa Terribile) and "The Warrior Pope" (Il Papa Guerriero), he set out with a courage and determination rarely equaled to rid himself of the various powers under which his temporal authority was challenged.[7] In 1506 he founded the Swiss Guard to provide a constant corps of soldiers to protect him. Meanwhile, in England the silver shilling of 1504 was the first English coin to be minted bearing a recognizable portrait of the king (Henry VII).[8] Then, another quintessential "Me" king takes the throne just six years after this Zenith:

CC Image

Henry VIII. Need we say more?

NOTE: About a decade after this Zenith of this "Me," during that time when Alpha Voices of literature and technology emerged and heralded the coming fulcrum, *Martin Luther posted his ninety-five theses* on the door of the church at Wittenberg Castle. His announcement that the people had direct access to God and did not require the facilitation of a priest may be the most pivotal and far-reaching Alpha Voice to date. From this "We" announcement, the Protestant movement emerged, and this would ultimately launch the Pilgrims and the Puritans to America. Wow.

An angry pope, a wanton king, and a fierce writer with a chip on his shoulder—I wonder how this is going to turn out.

1583 CE: *Queen Elizabeth* was at the peak of her power, having supported the establishment of an English Protestant church, of which she made herself the supreme governor. Her Navy will defeat the Spanish Armada just five years after this Zenith. This Zenith was the golden heart of England's Golden Age. William Shakespeare and Christopher Marlowe were rocking the nation with wit and humor while adventurers like Sir Francis Drake were dazzling it with their heroic exploits.

I'm as great a sovereign as any man.

1663 CE: *Charles II*, King of England, just two years prior to the Zenith of the "Me," shoved the *Corporation Act* through Parliament to strengthen his power. This act allowed Charles to remove anyone from office who was even suspected of being disloyal to him. In the years preceding the English Civil War many Royalists ("Me") had been removed from office and replaced by men loyal to Parliament ("We"). The Corporation Act reversed all this and gave unprecedented power to "Me" King Charles II.

If I even *think* you might disagree with me, you're outta here.

1743 CE: Young *Benjamin Franklin* made himself an entrepreneurial success and a celebrity in America through his publication of *Poor Richard's Almanac* from December 28, 1732 (eleven years prior to the Zenith), to 1758 (fifteen years past the Zenith, but still in the "Me"). Franklin then published the essay "The Way to Wealth." He was famous for walking around naked inside his home and is the author of the famous essays, "Fart Proudly," "Advice to a Young Man on the Choice of a Mistress," and "Rules on Making Oneself Disagreeable." Had he been born in the middle of the twentieth century, Franklin would no doubt have been a pot-smoking, live-and-let-live hippie. He said,

> **Any fool can criticize, condemn, and complain, and most fools do.**

1823 CE: *The Monroe Doctrine* announced that America had risen to its full height and would not tolerate interference in the Western hemisphere. President James Monroe proclaimed, "The American continents, by the free and independent condition which they have assumed and maintain, are henceforth not to be considered as subjects for future colonization by any European powers." In addition, the United States accepted the responsibility of being the protector of independent Western nations. Is that the ultimate "Me" announcement or what? Monroe was effectively saying,

> **The United States just wants to drink milk and kick ass, and we're all out of milk.**

1903 CE: *Teddy "Speak softly and carry a big stick" Roosevelt* was president. A classic "Me" hero, Teddy had already led the Rough Riders on a heroic charge up San Juan Hill in the Spanish-American War of 1898. He was the force behind the completion of the Panama Canal. His Great White Fleet was the first display of American military power, and when Roosevelt stepped in to negotiate an end to the Russo-Japanese War, he was awarded the Nobel Peace Prize. America had not yet invented action figures of comic book heroes, so we invented the "teddy" bear in his honor and carved his grinning face on Mount Rushmore.

In November 1899, when Teddy was returning from San Juan Hill to take his place in the Oval Office, Sigmund Freud published *The Interpretation of Dreams*. Freud favored free association as a tool for helping the mentally ill and believed repression to be the source of all mental illness. In what is perhaps the most sweeping "Me" statement of the century, Freud effectively claimed that duty, obligation, and conformity are the cause of every mental illness."

The colorful *Oscar Wilde* also made his name during the Upswing of this "Me," saying, "A man who does not think for himself does not think at all," and "The only way to get rid of temptation is to yield to it."

1983 CE: Very near this Zenith, *President Ronald Reagan* stood at the Berlin Wall, pointed to it, looked into the TV cameras, and boldly spoke a private message to the leader of the Soviet Union while the whole world was listening: "Mr. Gorbachev, tear down this wall." Wow. That's a true "Me" hero. In 1980, just a few years prior to this "Me" Zenith, the US Army unleashed its most powerful and enduring slogan: "Be All You Can Be." Army recruiters rode that slogan like a show pony while Reagan waved the Red, White, and Blue higher than it had ever been waved.

Twenty-one years later, just two years before the tipping point that would mark the end of this "Me," the Army realized "Be All You Can Be" was no longer performing like it once did, but they misunderstood the reason for this decline. Not understanding the motivations of a "We," the Army dropped "Be All You Can Be" in favor of the even more "Me" focused "Army of One." The results were disastrous. Just two years after the tipping point into "We," the now-frantic market researchers informed the Army that the slogan "Army of One" was contrary to the idea of teamwork and that potential recruits were now inexplicably drawn to the idea of being a productive member of a team. Accompanied by images of people working together, "Army Strong" became the new slogan, and recruitment began to improve.

2063: We can only imagine. (And we do, in a later chapter).

— 149 —

Pendulum Legend

Welcome to the Downswing of "Me." Think of it as a hot-air balloon
that begins to descend as its air begins to cool.

CHAPTER FIFTEEN

1983–2003:
The Twenty-Year
Downswing from "Me"

1985: We're only two years past the Zenith of "Me" and we're already reminiscing about the glory years of the Upswing (1963–1973). Bruce Springsteen haunted us with a song,

Glory days! Well, they'll pass you by.
Glory days! In the wink of a young girl's eye.
Glory days . . . glory days.

1989: Seeing our need to re-create the glory days from our past, Mazda studies the quintessential British sports cars of yesterday, including two Lotus Elans, as part of their process in designing the hugely successful Mazda MX-5 Miata. The Japanese convertible re-created the road feel, the exhaust sound, and the geometry between seat, stick shift, and steering wheel.

We saw a photo of a young man in Norway cradling a racing helmet in his lap as he sat cross-legged on the trunk of his new Miata convertible. This was his online post:

I grew up in a period dominated by history's greatest sports cars: Jaguar E-type, Austin Healey, MGB and Lotus Elan, to mention some. When I decided to buy a sports car, I knew what I wanted: a nimble, rear-wheel drive roadster with good

handling, twin-cam engine, and good design. A Lotus Elan type of car but without the hassle. The MX5 / Miata was a natural choice![1]

Think about it: he's driving a car with an engine the size of a loaf of bread and dreaming about the powerful Jaguar V12s of yesterday. His little econo-box lacks the power to pull a fat kid off the toilet, but he's certain he needs that helmet *because he's a racecar man.*

Welcome to the Downswing of "Me." Think of it as a hot-air balloon that begins to descend as its air begins to cool.

Generation X was never an age group; it was an attitude—the cooling of the hot-air balloon of "Me."

Figure 15.1 Downswing from a Zenith of "ME."

Figure 15.2 Values of "ME" Zenith when society takes a good thing too far.

ZENITH CHARACTERISTICS	ME

TAKING THINGS TOO FAR

GET ALL YOU CAN. CAN ALL YOU GET. SIT ON THE CAN. POISON THE REST.
HE WHO DIES WITH THE MOST TOYS WINS.

- Individuality disintegrates into a costume party
- Big hair, disco, and glam rock
- Branding campaigns are "costume parties"

- Advertising—promises that businesses have no intention of keeping
- Literature: fantasy, terror, and heroes
- Winning is all that matters.
- Recreating the glory days

1993: Halfway Down a "Me"

We've arrived once again at year thirty in a forty-year window. It's time to listen for the Alpha Voices of technology and literature that will open our eyes to a new reality that will become mainstream in just ten short years. This time, technology and literature arrive in the same package.

March 19, 1992

AOL went public on the NASDAQ, offering two million shares for $11.50 each.

October 8, 1992

Walt Mossberg wrote in an article about online services for the *Wall Street Journal:* "I see America Online as the sophisticated wave of the future."

January, 1993

AOL launches a Windows version, with links to graphics.

July, 1993

AOL floods America with discs in the mail. You remember, don't you? You couldn't open a box of cereal or the seatback pocket in front of you without pulling out a free CD that would install America Online on your hard drive.

"You've got mail. You've got mail. You've got mail. You've got mail. You've got mail. You've got . . . "

America Online's ease of installation and automatic start-up caused it to become wildly successful with both the public as well as investors.

This dot-com bubble would burst, of course, because this was merely the Alpha Voice ten years ahead of reality. The bandwidth limitations imposed by 54 kbps dial-up modems made it impossible for the Internet to deliver streaming video. Even simple Flash animations on home pages took several minutes to download. Not only were there no effective search engines; there was nothing to search for even if there had been. The web was essentially e-mail and chat rooms. Your inbox was clogged each day with multiple copies of the same jokes and stories forwarded from all your friends.

The most notable survivor of the dot-com bubble burst was Amazon.com. Created by Jeff Bezos in 1994, Amazon's searchable content grew exponentially compared to other sites, and its pages weren't burdened with gimmicks that took a long time to load.

It's interesting to note that popular music at the halfway point of a Downswing will usually sound just like the music at the halfway point of the Upswing twenty years before. This is due to the fact that popular music reflects the desires of the masses, and the Pendulum is in precisely the same position when it is halfway down as when it is halfway up.

As we moved forward from the Halfway-Up position of 1973, music got slick, tight, polished, and choreographed as we approached the "Me" Zenith (1983) and entered the "disco" phase. But now that the Pendulum of 1993 has returned to the same position it occupied in 1973, popular music "sounds like 1973 all over again." Listen for yourself and see if you don't agree.

Figure 15.3 Popular music themes in a downswing from a "ME" Zenith.

POPULAR MUSIC THEMES: DOWNSWING FROM "ME" (1993)	ME

"WHAT BEGAN IN JOY ENDS IN BONDAGE"

1993:

1. "(I Can't Help) Falling in Love with You," UB40

MESSAGE

Wise men say, 'Only fools rush in.' But I can't help falling in love with you.	**I am irresistibly attracted to you.**

2. "I'd Do Anything for Love (But I Won't Do That)," Meat Loaf

I would do anything for love, but I won't do that. No, I won't do that.	**I love you, but let's not forget— I'm really in this for me.**

3. "Informer," Snow

They have no clues and they wanna get warmer, But Shan won't turn informer.	**I know who I am and I am true to myself.**

4. "What's Up?" 4 Non Blondes

Twenty-five years of my life and still Trying to get up that great big hill of hope for a destination	**I'm searching for the meaning of everything.**

5. "All That She Wants," Ace of Base

So if you are in sight and the day is right, She's a hunter. You're the fox.	**A woman is hungry for you.**

1997

Strauss and Howe follow up their *Generations* with a sequel called *The Fourth Turning*. At one point in the book, they speak of the United States at the "We" Zenith of 1943 and compare it to 1997—the year when they're writing—when America was just beginning to emerge from more than three decades of "Me." They state,

ME Around World War II, we were proud as a people, but modest as individuals. Where we once thought ourselves collectively strong, we now regard ourselves as individually entitled. . . . Fewer than 2 people in 10 said yes when asked, 'Are you a very important person?' Today more than six in 10 say yes.[2]

And now it's 1998.

Forty years have passed since that new style of music called rock and roll began to make its way into the mainstream. The time has come again for a new musical genre to begin nudging its way into mix. Following the Alpha Voices of 1958, we had top-forty Rock, Bubblegum Rock, Hard Rock, Soft Rock, Punk Rock, Grunge Rock, Album Rock, Country Rock, and Instrumental Rock.

Whatever this new music is, we know it won't be just another variation of rock.

Ever heard of rap and hip hop?

Just as it was in 1958, the top three songs of 1998 are the "old" style of music that would soon begin to fade. But there it was again at number four . . . our first Alpha Voice in the Top 100. This has to be a coincidence, right? Again just as before, a solid thirty of the Top 100 are clearly rap or hip hop, and another dozen lean gently toward it while keeping the other foot planted safely in rock and roll.

Like rock and roll, rap was pioneered by African Americans, but taken mainstream by a white boy. Eminem, the white popularizer of rap, said in an early interview,

WE My insecurities? I'm dumb, I'm stupid, I'm white, I'm ugly, I smell, and I'm white . . . I wanna kill myself . . . My nose is crooked . . . um, my penis is small.

Self-effacing transparency is utterly disarming, is it not?

Rap and hip hop don't top the list in 1998, but we weren't yet at the tipping point, either.

Figure 15.4   Alpha voices in music leading into a "WE" cycle.

WE TOP 100 SONGS OF 1998: ALPHA VOICES IN MUSIC BEGIN TO EMERGE ME

1. **"My Heart Will Go On,"** Celine Dion

2. **"Believe,"** Cher

3. **"I Don't Want to Miss a Thing,"** Aerosmith

4. **"The Boy Is Mine,"** Brandy & Monica—*rap/hip hop*

5. **"Frozen,"** Madonna—*rap/hip hop*

6. **"Torn,"** Natalie Imbruglia

7. **"It's Like That,"** Run DMC & Jason Nevins—*rap/hip hop*

8. **"Big Big World,"** Emilia—*rap/hip hop*

9. **"Truly Madly Deeply,"** Savage Garden—*rap/hip hop*

10. **"Together Again,"** Janet Jackson—*rap/hip hop*

11. **"Ghetto Supastar,"** Pras Michel—*rap/hip hop*

12. **"Iris,"** The Goo Goo Dolls

13. **"Never Ever,"** All Saints—*rap/hip hop*

14. **"Crush,"** Jennifer Paige—*rap/hip hop*

15. **"Life,"** Des'ree—*rap/hip hop*

16. **"No Matter What,"** Boyzone

17. **"When You Believe,"** Mariah Carey & Whitney Houston—*rap/hip hop*

18. **"Gettin' Jiggy wit It,"** Will Smith—*rap/hip hop*

19. **"All My Life,"** K-Ci & JoJo—*rap/hip hop*

20. **"Viva Forever,"** Spice Girls—*rap/hip hop*

21. **"Goodbye,"** Spice Girls—*rap/hip hop*

22. **"Doo Wop (That Thing),"** Lauryn Hill—*rap/hip hop*

23. **"Doctor Jones,"** Aqua—*rap/hip hop*

24. **"Ray of Light,"** Madonna—*rap/hip hop*

25. **"High,"** The Lighthouse Family—*rap/hip hop*

26. **"The Sweetest Thing,"** U2

27. **"Thank U,"** Alanis Morissette

28. **"You're Still the One,"** Shania Twain

29. **"Come with Me,"** P Diddy & Jimmy Page—*rap/hip hop*

30. **"La Copa de La Vida,"** Ricky Martin—*rap/hip hop*

31. **"C'est la Vie,"** B*Witched—*rap/hip hop*

32. **"Save Tonight,"** Eagle-Eye Cherry

33. **"God Is a DJ,"** Faithless—*rap/hip hop*

34. **"Angels,"** Robbie Williams

35. **"Everything's Gonna Be Alright,"** Sweetbox

36. **"I'm Your Angel,"** Celine Dion & R Kelly

37. **"When You're Gone,"** Bryan Adams & Melanie C

38. **"Millennium,"** Robbie Williams

39. **"All I Have to Give,"** The Backstreet Boys—*rap/hip hop*

40. **"Hard Knock Life,"** Jay-Z—*rap/hip hop*

41. **"Flugzeuge im Bauch,"** Oli P—*rap/hip hop*

42. **"Intergalactic,"** The Beastie Boys—*rap/hip hop*

43. **"Turn It Up, Fire It Up,"** Busta Rhymes—*rap/hip hop*

44. **"Cherish,"** Pappa Bear—*rap/hip hop*

45. **"Music Sounds Better with You,"** Stardust—*rap/hip hop*

46. **"The Power of Good-Bye,"** Madonna—*rap/hip hop*

47. **"Too Much,"** Spice Girls—*rap/hip hop*

48. **"Immortality,"** Celine Dion & Bee Gees

49. **"My All,"** Mariah Carey—*rap/hip hop*

50. **"The Cup of Life,"** Ricky Martin—*rap/hip hop*

51. **"The Way,"** Fastball

52. **"9pm (Till I Come),"** ATB—*rap/hip hop*

53. **"Too Close,"** Next—*rap/hip hop*

54. **"Stand by Me,"** 4 the Cause—*rap/hip hop*

55. **"Feel It,"** Tamperer—*rap/hip hop*

56. **"Time of Your Life (Good Riddance),"** Green Day

57. **"Bailando,"** Loona—*rap/hip hop*

58. **"One Week,"** Barenaked Ladies

59. **"How Deep Is Your Love?"** Dru Hill—*rap/hip hop*

60. **"Sex & Candy,"** Marcy Playground

61. **"Deeper Underground,"** Jamiroquai

62. **"This Kiss,"** Faith Hill

63. **"Rollercoaster,"** B*Witched—*rap/hip hop*

64. **"Outside,"** George Michael—*rap/hip hop*

65. **"Stop,"** Spice Girls—*rap/hip hop*

66. **"Hands,"** Jewel

67. **"Tragedy,"** Steps—*rap/hip hop*

68. **"Only When I Lose Myself,"** Depeche Mode

69. **"La Primavera,"** Sash!—*rap/hip hop*

70. **"All Around the World,"** Oasis

71. **"My Favorite Mistake,"** Sheryl Crow

72. **"If You Tolerate This Your Children Will Be Next,"** The Manic Street Preachers

73. **"Everybody Get Up,"** Five—*rap/hip hop*

74. **"Carnival de Paris,"** Dario G—*rap/hip hop*

75. **"Mysterious Times,"** Sash! & Tina Cousins—*rap/hip hop*

76. **"Hijo de la luna,"** Loona—*rap/hip hop*

77. **"Life Is a Flower"** Ace of Base

78. **"My Favourite Game,"** The Cardigans

79. **"Would You . . . ?"** Touch & Go—*rap/hip hop*

Sister photography

80. **"Are You That Somebody?"** Aaliyah—*rap/hip hop*

81. **"Walkin' on the Sun,"** Smash Mouth

82. **"Adia,"** Sarah McLachlan

83. **"Horny '98,"**——Mousse T & Hot 'n Juicy—*rap/hip hop*

84. **"Open Your Eyes,"** Guano Apes

85. **"My Oh My,"** Aqua—*rap/hip hop*

86. **"All 'Bout the Money,"** Meja

87. **"How Much Is the Fish?"** Scooter—*rap/hip hop*

88. **"No No No,"** Destiny's Child—*rap/hip hop*

89. **"Under the Bridge,"** All Saints

90. **"No Tengo Dinero,"** Los Umbrellos

91. **"My Father's Eyes,"** Eric Clapton

92. **"Brimful of Asha,"** Cornershop

93. **"The Rockafeller Skank,"** Fatboy Slim

94. **"When the Lights Go Out,"** Five

95. **"The First Night,"** Monica—*rap/hip hop*

96. **"Just the Two of Us,"** Will Smith—*rap/hip hop*

97. **"5–6-7–8,"** Steps

98. **"Rescue Me,"** Bell Book & Candle

99. **"From This Moment On,"** Shania Twain

100. **"Laura non c'l,"** Nek

Matt Gibbons

1999

During this year, Chris Locke, Doc Searls, David Weinberger, and Rick Levine posted online "The Cluetrain Manifesto." Their ninety-five theses were as revolutionary as the ninety-five theses Martin Luther posted on the door of Wittenberg Castle Church in 1517. Their statements and conclusions may seem self-evident today, but they were considered crazy talk back in 1999. Here are four of the ninety-five:

3. Conversations among human beings *sound* human. They are conducted in a human voice.

4. Whether delivering information, opinions, perspectives, dissenting arguments or humorous asides, the human voice is typically open, natural, uncontrived.

15. In just a few more years, the current homogenized "voice" of business—the sound of mission statements and brochures—will seem as contrived and artificial as the language of the eighteenth-century French court.

22. Having a sense of humor does not mean putting some jokes on the corporate website; rather, it requires big values, a little humility, straight talk, and a genuine point of view.

Figure 15.5 Key points from the Cluetrain Manifesto that you can apply in online conversations.

KEY POINTS FROM THE CLUETRAIN MANIFESTO	ME

HOW TO HAVE "HUMAN TO HUMAN" CONVERSATIONS ONLINE

1. Talk like a human. Conversations *sound* human.

2. Sound human by being open, natural, and uncontrived in all conversations.

3. Ditch the standard homogenized "voice" of business. Mission statements and brochures sound artificial.

4. Big values, a little humility, straight talk, and a genuine point of view sell. Corny jokes on the corporate website don't cut it.

"Putting some jokes on the corporate website" sounds absurd, right? But this was a typical response of business owners in 1999 when the staff finished their brainstorming about "how to create a website that people might like to visit." After all, jokes and stories are what clogged our inboxes, remember?

WE Self-effacing transparency is utterly disarming.
—*Michael R. Drew*

Anyone in 1999 who was advising advertisers to embrace "humility, straight talk, and a genuine point of view" was speaking a language that was completely foreign to mainstream business. Society was still in a "Me," and the tipping point was yet four years away.

Do you remember Mike Myers in the movie *Austin Powers?* Awakened from a twenty-five-year sleep, this ultrasuave, parody character of James Bond is told, "The Cold War is over."

Austin replies, "Well, finally those capitalist pigs will pay for their crimes, eh? Eh, comrades? Eh?"

"Austin, we won."

"Oh, groovy, smashing, yea, capitalism. . ."

At one point in the movie the villainous Dr. Evil announces, "I'm going to place him in an easily escapable situation involving an overly elaborate and exotic death . . . Alright guard, begin the unnecessarily slow-moving dipping mechanism."

Austin Powers was blatant mockery of James Bond, the ultimate hero of the "Me" that was winding down. The *Austin Powers* movies (1997–2002) were wildly successful, bringing in over $676 million at the box office, plus additional revenues from DVDs.

All the Alpha Voices whispered the same message as society approached the tipping point of 2003: "We want the truth, even if it's ugly. Shrink-wrapped, sugar-coated, phony posing is no longer acceptable."

Pendulum Legend

"Would you cut the crap, Mom and Dad? Seriously! Just
give it to me straight. You're treating me like a five-year-old!
I'm eleven, dammit."

CHAPTER SIXTEEN

2003–2023: The Twenty-Year Upswing into "We" One More Time

You may recall that our adventure began in Chapter 1 with the words, "Nick, we just finished 1963 all over again, but this time we're headed in the opposite direction."

Had I fully understood the alternating directions of society's forty-year Pendulum, I might have more accurately said, "Nick, 2003 was 1923 all over again. Same position. Same direction."

The "Monday Morning Memo" for January 13, 2003:

Figure 16.1   The first half of an upswing into "WE"

Year of the Internet's Bar Mitzvah

During the second half of the 1990s the first hand in the air following every public session I taught would be followed by the question, "What about the Internet?"

My answer never changed: "The Internet is a baby born prematurely. It will grow up to become everything you've been promised, but it can't possibly happen as quickly as they're saying."

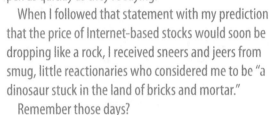

When I followed that statement with my prediction that the price of Internet-based stocks would soon be dropping like a rock, I received sneers and jeers from smug, little reactionaries who considered me to be "a dinosaur stuck in the land of bricks and mortar."

Remember those days?

Then, in January of 2001, reporter Rich Kyanka wrote, "If you've heard news regarding any online networks lately, their name was more than likely followed by details of massive layoffs, delayed payments, breaches of contract, or even their imminent demise. . . . Why has Internet advertising failed? . . . Despite all the intensely positive predictions and glorious outlooks to the future, something suddenly went wrong. Investors began demanding to know where all their money was going and when they'd get to see their cash return. Suddenly the business plan of having no business plan began to taste sour. Companies refused to sink further funding into an industry that was essentially founded on smoke and mirrors. The lure of having your name attached to a dot-com began to seem less and less appealing, and investors began to pull out at unbelievable speeds. . . . Simply put, the current [Internet] advertising model does not work. Readers know this, companies know this, and online advertisers definitely know this. Advertisers, whom the entire Internet is funded by, need things that aren't currently being offered."

Longtime readers of these "Monday Morning Memos" will recall that during a year after high-tech's crash of the NASDAQ I wrote to you saying, "Make no mistake. I still believe that the Internet will ultimately deliver all that it promised, but not quite yet. . . . I'll tell you when it's time to get in.

Figure 16.2 Drivers of a "WE" cycle.

WE — DRIVERS OF A "WE" CYCLE

WHAT'S ON THE HORIZON?

1. Conforms for the common good
2. Assumes personal responsibility
3. Believes a million men are wiser than one man
4. Yearns to create a better world—"I came, I saw, *I concurred.*"
5. Takes small actions
6. Desires to be part of a productive team
7. Values humility and thoughtful persons
8. Believes leadership is "This is the problem as I see it. Let's solve it together."
9. Focuses on solving problems to strengthen society's sense of purpose

Now Is That Time

The buying public has finally figured out what the Internet is currently best suited for—information gathering and features-based comparison shopping. A recent report by *Reuters* indicates that 79 percent of today's Internet users expect businesses to have a website and for that site "to give them information about products that they are considering buying."

The Internet is no longer a new and strange phenomenon. America has grown accustomed to it, and we're turning to it for information with increasing regularity. According to Google.com, more than fifty-five billion searches were conducted on their search engine alone last year, and nearly eighty million searches "of a commercial nature" are being conducted each day. This is a number equal to about one-third of the total US population. And that's a *daily* number.

Your customers are among those conducting these "commercial searches." Is your information there for them to find? Without question, 2003 is the year for business owners to get serious about their Internet presence; but here are some important things that you should know:

Figure 16.3 Mindset and values in society during a "WE" cycle.

WE

TIPS TO CREATE A SERIOUS INTERNET PRESENCE IN A WE CYCLE

1. Informative is the jumbo jet that will take you where you want to go.

2. The web is an information delivery system. Not an advertising vehicle.

3. Use your site to build confidence, inform your customer and anticipate and answer questions 24/7.

4. Insightful website architecture and exceptional writing tromp dazzling graphics.

5. Make it easy on your customers. Frustrate them and they're gone.

 I never jump on bandwagons, but instead, always wait for the armored car that hauls the money. The Internet bandwagon crashed and burned in 2000. Now is the year of the armored car.
Are you ready to ride?

—Roy H. Williams

Like any accurate prediction, my assertion in January 2003, that "Now is that time" seems self-evident. But keep in mind the Internet was still something of a wasteland at that time. Very few people had heard of Wikipedia. Google was still struggling with its business model, and PayPal™ was looking for early adopters. Facebook hadn't been launched yet, and YouTube was still three years away. Twitter was barely on the horizon, four years in the future.

As we moved into the six-year transitional window of 2003 to 2008, the Pendulum was in the same position it held in 1923, at the beginning of the last "We." The top songs in a "We" are never the "apple trees and honey bees and snow-white turtle doves" of a "Me." Do you remember the whining and complaining lyrics of 1923 as Western society embraced cold, hard facts and reveled in the pain of clear-eyed reality?

Figure 16.4 Popular music themes in a downswing from a "WE" cycle.

WE POPULAR MUSIC THEMES: FIRST HALF OF AN UPSWING INTO "WE" (2003–2013)

2003'S TOP SONGS

	MESSAGE
1. "Where Is the Love?" The Black Eyed Peas	
What's wrong with the world, mama?	**People don't practice what**
Selfishness got us followin' our wrong direction.	**they preach.**
2. "Hey Ya!" OutKast	
My baby don't mess around because she loves me so.	**I'm not as sure as I want to be.**
And this I know for sho. But does she really wanna?	
3. "All the Things She Said"—t.A.T.u.	
I'm in serious shit, I feel totally lost	**I'm confused and unsure of**
And I'm all mixed up, feeling cornered and rushed.	**what to do.**
4. "Shut Up," The Black Eyed Peas	
And we try to make it work	**We try and try, but we just can't**
But it still ends up the worst.	**get along.**

The year 2003 was the year the Hollywood movie formula was turned on its head. Motion picture studios had long known that all they had to do to ensure a movie's success was to pair the hot leading man of the moment—at that time, Ben Affleck—with the hot leading lady of the moment—Jennifer Lopez—and fan the flames of a tabloid romance. Then release a movie starring the love-struck pair and—*ka-ching!*—watch the money roll in. Hollywood worked this formula perfectly in 2003. Ben gave Jennifer an engagement ring with a six-carat, pink diamond worth $1.2 million, and the pair were photographed together *everywhere.*

The movie they made, *Gigli,* was released in 2,215 theaters on August 1, a Friday. Ticket sales were down 27 percent the next day, and by Sunday the movie was deader than a bag of hammers.[1]

Gigli was pulled from theaters on August 21, having taken in only slightly more than $7 million worldwide. Unfortunately, that movie cost $54 million to produce.

A two-word text is all it takes to stand Hollywood on its head and bring a movie to its knees: "Gigli sucks."

Lesson learned: *blog posts and e-mail can quickly counter promotional hype.*

Like a mighty ocean wave, a second text pushed a different movie far beyond where it was expected to go. This movie came out on a Wednesday, and ticket sales jumped 19 percent the next day.[2] By Friday a ticket to this movie was impossible to find. "Pirates rock" was all it took. *Pirates of the Caribbean* remained in theaters worldwide for more than six months and brought in more than $654 million. Johnny Depp's four-movie franchise about a not-dangerous pirate who acts like a semi-drunk Keith Richards is currently at $3.8 billion and climbing. Consider the clash of perspectives during a six-year transitionary window: a "Me" is about dreams, possibilities, positive thinking, and inspiration, whereas a "We" is about small actions, consequences, realistic appraisals, and damage control. These very different outlooks led to an interesting series of exchanges between slow-to-change parents and their quick-changing children during the transitionary window that followed the tipping point of 2003.

A new college graduate sent out her résumé and received an invitation to be interviewed for a job in another state. She asked her "Me" generation parents for an airplane ticket and was told, "Honey, you just tell them that if they want the best, they're just going to have to send you a plane ticket. You need to make these people understand how special you are."

Her parents weren't tightfisted and stingy; they just didn't realize that the workplace was no longer catering to the posturing delusions of "Me." Her parents were sharing what was once traditional wisdom, not realizing that times had changed.

Do you remember the weird exchanges triggered when parents tried to soft-sell their children? "Would you cut the crap, Mom and

Dad? Seriously! Just give it to me straight. Quit trying to sugarcoat it. You're treating me like a five-year-old! I'm eleven, dammit."

Here's the "Monday Morning Memo" that this conflict of perspectives triggered:

Opie Don't Live in Mayberry No More

Childhood's innocent mischief is nearing extinction—an unanticipated side effect of the explosion in technology. Tom Sawyer and Huck Finn have become dusty icons of an earlier society. Today's kids are finding it difficult to relate to the drawings of Norman Rockwell; most have never sat at that Thanksgiving table, played marbles with those neighborhood kids, or skinny-dipped in that swimmin' hole.

Have you watched cartoons on TV lately? The level of social satire in cartoons targeted to six-year-olds would astound you. Ambushed by unexpected adulthood, children are being robbed of the carefree days that would have rooted them in reality and sustained them with a lifetime of memories.

Today's kids are a savvy, streetwise generation that was never given a chance to be naïve.

But the techno-explosion that robbed them of their childhood also empowered them to stay connected. A new message is being whispered, and we had better take it seriously: "Your advertising may fool one of us. But that one will tell the rest of us."

Word-of-mouth has grown into the muscular beast, interconnectivity, and it moves with lightning speed. Cell phones and e-mail are rewriting the rules of commerce. Online chat-rooms, blogs, and instant messaging are ensuring that whether good or bad, the word gets out.

We're moving into an era of transparency in which it will become harder than ever to win new customers through hype alone. We're beginning to hear the sound of the new branding, and it's the sound of "real." Today's hunger is for reality and truth.

I think Carl Rogers said it best when he said, "What I am is good enough, if only I would be it openly."[3]

And what you are is good enough too.

Be it openly.

—*Roy H. Williams*

Figure 16.5 Tips to create a serious Internet presence during a "WE" cycle.

WE	UPSWING INTO "WE"	
VALUES	**REJECTS**	
• Authenticity	• Hype	
• Teamwork	• Posing	
• Humility	• Arrogance	
• Small actions	• Wishful thinking	
• Personal responsibility	• Self-righteousness	
• Cold, hard truth	• Sugar-coated B.S.	

Paul Townsend

WE Remember L'Oréal's famous "Me" slogan, "Because I'm worth it?" As society passed the tipping point of 2003 and the "Me" became fully unwound, the old slogan was replaced with "Because you're worth it."

Figure 16.6 Popular movie themes in an upswing into a "WE" cycle.

WE — POPULAR MOVIE THEMES IN UPSWING TO "WE"

WORKING TOGETHER FOR THE COMMON GOOD

Fight Club (1999)	MESSAGE
A depressed young man becomes a cog in the wheel of big business. Don't put stock in the materialistic world. One can learn a lot through pain, misfortune, and chaos.	**You ain't all that dog, you ain't all that. We are the all-singing, all-dancing crap of the world.**
8 Mile (2002)	
A Rosetta Stone. Young, frustrated, blue-collar worker transcends meager beginnings and rises from a trailer to millionaire rapster.	**I'm not perfect. I have problems. Money and fame don't turn life into a "happily ever after."**
Lost in Translation (2003)	
Boy meets girl, they fall in love, and true love doesn't prevail in the end.	**Sometimes love hurts because you have to deny your feelings and do the right thing.**
Pirates of the Caribbean (2003)	
A story about misfits who can't succeed alone and who show they are all equal in finding success.	**Working together is the only way to get what we want.**
Napoleon Dynamite (2004)	
Weird misfits can be happy too.	**Are yesterday's losers the winners of tomorrow?**
Juno (2006)	
Teenage girl deals with pregnancy and the harsh realities of life and the bumps along the way.	**Teen pregnancy is a reality. Deal with it.**
Little Miss Sunshine (2007)	
A tragically funny (and realistic) look into the world of child pageants.	**Dysfunction is okay. We can still solve problems if we work together.**

In 2006, the fourth year of the six-year transitionary window, a discussion thread appeared on Harmony Central Forums:

Because You Deserve It!

Is anybody else as irritated by this line of marketing as I am? I swear that every time I listen to the radio or turn on commercial TV, I get inundated with ads telling me that I deserve 200 channels of television, I deserve-wrinkle-free skin, I deserve to eat at the best place in town, I deserve to drive a luxury vehicle, I deserve perfect children, I deserve to live in a mansion, I deserve perfect health, etc., etc., etc. . . .

Is this line of marketing indicative of deeper societal issues?

As far as I'm concerned, I don't deserve shit save only two things: that which I have earned through hard work and sacrifice, and that which I have paid for with money earned from my hard work and sacrifice.

Am I right in my thinking or just old and cranky?

All the readers who left a comment agreed with this post. No one thought he or she was just old and cranky. "Yes, hard work and sacrifice deserve our praise! Hard work and sacrifice! Hooray!": society is definitely in a "We" again.

In 2008, we saw the implosion of an American economy created during a "Me." Although it is dangerous to make specific predictions regarding the economy or a political election based on the swinging of society's Pendulum, it is reasonable to recognize that during the six-year transitionary window into a "We" (2003–2008), society will begin to demand increased transparency within the system. This usually leads to alarm when we realize how truly absurd the system has become, and it's not unusual that a recession will mark the transition from "Me" to "We."

 Coauthor Michael R. Drew spoke at length to author Harry Dent Jr., whose books on economic theory seem to indicate that a recession/depression will always occur at the beginning of every "We" cycle. (Coauthor Roy H. Williams is less convinced than Michael R. Drew, but Williams is old and cranky.)

In 2009, at the end of the six-year transition, consumer psychologist Dr. Maxim Titorenko convinced L'Oréal to change their famous slogan to "Because *we're* worth it." Nice try, L'Oréal, but you still sound a tiny bit full of yourself.

2010: A single website, *amazon.com*, brought in more than $34 billion. That's more than $93 million a day, nearly $1 million every fifteen minutes. YouTube is the second most widely used website next to Google, and 750 million people exchange information each day on Facebook. The Internet is finally delivering everything it promised during the dot-com bubble fifteen years earlier.

HubSpot reports that 24 percent of adults have posted a review of a product they have purchased. This means that one of every four customers believes enough in online reviews that they've gone to the trouble to post one themselves. Have you ever posted an online review?

2011: L'Oréal hired Hugh Laurie (aka, Dr. Gregory House) to be their spokesperson. In the first video posted on YouTube, Laurie mocks the idea of cosmetics for men while at the same time making it seem perfectly natural. At one point in the video he says, "It's an interesting question to pose: 'Because you're worth it.' I hope I am, I hope I am. I hope you are. I hope we *all* are."

Gutsy move, L'Oréal. Hugh Laurie plays a self-centered "Me" dinosaur as Dr. Gregory House. To have him evolve on camera into a charming and self-effacing "We" spokesman is a brilliant stroke of casting. Whether or not the public will accept it as credible has yet to be seen.

The June 6 cover of the *New Yorker* featured an illustration of three citizens with their heads and hands in stocks, being punished as though in colonial times. The sign above one man says, "smoking." The sign above the woman next to him says "salt." Another man's sign says "carbs."

It would appear we're becoming judgmental and self-righteous again, right on schedule, halfway up a "We."

iStockphoto / drbimages

The June 13 issue of the *New Yorker* featured the cartoon of a rather bewildered superhero (p. 103). The caption said, "Able to leap tall buildings because he should, because it's the right thing to do, and because he would feel guilty if he didn't."

When the covers of magazines reflect sanctimonious judgmentalism and we can identify with cartoons about being riddled with guilt, our society is most definitely in a "We." Magazines in a "Me" have heroic figures on their covers, and their cartoons are about ego and superficiality.

These examples are just a few of the thousands that are all around you. Look at any magazine, TV show, or movie; read any best-selling book; listen to the most popular hit songs—and then decide for yourself if what we're telling you is true.

"Is the Rock Format Dead?" In July, 2011, *Radio Ink* magazine quoted a story that had appeared in the *Chicago Tribune* the previous day, saying that Rock "is not the dominant sound that it was in the

'60s and '70s, when Rock really was the sound of a generation." The article went on to say that radio programmers who think "alternative Rock has eclipsed Bob Seger and Bruce Springsteen believe a fork should be stuck in 'the old-fart format' . . . Is it time to put the Led Zeppelin, Ted Nugent format to sleep for good?"

Pendulum Legend

Virtually every instance of widespread viciousness in Western society has happened within ten years of the Zenith of a "We." 2013–2033: Who will we burn this time?

—*Michael R. Drew*

CHAPTER SEVENTEEN

2013–2023:
What Happens Next?
A Discussion of Experts

Jaron Lanier is the Internet guru who popularized the term "Virtual Reality." In his book, *You Are Not a Gadget: A Manifesto,* he argued that online aggregators like Google, Amazon, iTunes, and YouTube help only themselves, not the little people who actually create the songs, books, and videos: "Wikipedia, a mediocre product of group writing, has become the intellectual backbone of the Web. We're treating aggregators of content as though they're more important than the actual creators of content."

Lanier argued that online aggregators are built on the theory that a million men are wiser than one man. *But individual genius is based*

Figure 17.1   The Zenith of a "WE" cycle.

on the assumption that one man is wiser than a million men. Lanier is a dissenting voice, representing the minority "Me" contingent that disagrees with society's current Upswing toward "We."

If this were 2033, Lanier would be an Alpha Voice, shining a hot spotlight on the new way of thinking that will become mainstream in 2043. We can only guess what new genre of music will be spawned in 2038, but you can be sure it will embody the core message that Lanier's *You Are Not a Gadget* trumpeted: "Genius is not a group project."[1]

Society will probably look back and see Lanier as a man ahead of his time. The words he wrote in 2010 will likely encapsulate the feelings of the majority in 2033, when our current "We" is at the halfway point of its Downswing.

Not surprisingly, Lanier's message is essentially what John Steinbeck shouted in 1952, when society's Pendulum was in precisely the same position, the halfway point of the Downswing of a "We."

> ## ME
> Nothing was ever created by two men. There are no good collaborations, whether in music, in art, in poetry, in mathematics, in philosophy. Once the miracle of creation has taken place, the group can build and extend it, but the group never invents anything. The preciousness lies in the lonely mind of a man.
>
> —*John Steinbeck*[2]

Steinbeck spoke of the glory and value of "Me," as did Lanier. A "Me" is a good thing, no question about it, but "Me" isn't where the majority of Western society is headed during the years 2013 to 2033. If history is a reliable guide, we're about to take a good thing too far. As we approach 2023, the Zenith of our current "We," we're about to learn what Steinbeck was talking about when he spoke of a similar time: "a teetotaler is not content not to drink—he must stop all the drinking in the world; a vegetarian among us would outlaw the eating of meat.

Yes, "working together for the common good" can quickly become self-righteousness. In the words of novelist David Farland, "Men who believe themselves to be good, who do not search their own souls, often commit the worst atrocities. A man who sees himself as evil will restrain himself. It is only when we do evil in the belief that we do good that we pursue it wholeheartedly."[3]

WE Working together for the common good can quickly become self-righteousness.

—Michael R. Drew

The decades that fall on each side of a Zenith are the twenty years when society is most out of balance and suffering for it. Conversely, the ten years that fall on each side of a tipping point are those decades when society is most in balance—between "Halfway Down" and "Halfway Up."

Balance: From halfway down a "We" to halfway up a "Me" is unicorns and rainbows, "I'm OK, you're OK," "Apple trees, honeybees, snow-white turtledoves!" "I'm going to buy the world a Coke!" (1953–1973).

Out of balance: From halfway up a "Me" to halfway down that "Me" is a time of hero worship, when we wish we were someone we admire. "I'm not OK, you're OK," Big hair and costumes, phony is the new real (1973–1993).

Balance: From halfway down a "Me" to halfway up a "We" is a time of mutual brokenness, transparency, and authenticity: "I'm screwed up, and you're screwed up, so let's both just forgive each other and look past all this, okay?" This season of "I'm not OK, you're not OK" feels a lot like "I'm OK, you're OK" because both seasons fall on the tipping points halfway between the Zeniths. Daniel Pink's book *Drive* points to this as precisely the time when we begin moving

iStockphoto / Thomas Vogel

from extrinsic motivators like big houses and cars to intrinsic motivators like autonomy, mastery, and purpose (1993–2013).

Out of balance: From halfway up a "We" to halfway down that "We" is the time of witch hunts, transparency, and authenticity: "I'm OK, you're not OK," the twenty-year season of Holy Wars, *us vs. them*. "We, the good and righteous defenders of truth and beauty against them, the evil and sinister malefactors intent on destroying our way of life" (2013–2033).

Figure 17.2 Balance and out of balance through time.

WE	BALANCE	ME

HALFWAY DOWN A "ME" TO HALFWAY UP A "WE"

Mutual brokenness

1993–2013

Moving from big houses and cars to autonomy, mastery, and purpose.

WE	HALFWAY UP A "WE" TO HALFWAY DOWN A "ME"

HALFWAY UP A "WE" TO HALFWAY DOWN A "WE"

Witch hunts

2013–2033

WE	BALANCE	ME

HALFWAY DOWN A "WE" TO HALFWAY UP A "ME"

Unicorns and Rainbows

1953–1973

Apple trees, honeybees, snow-white turtledoves. I'm going to buy the world a Coke!

Holy wars: *Us vs. Them*

Let's take a look at a few of the more infamous seasons of a "We" Zenith:

Figure 17.3 Balance: Tipping Point.

I'M O.K. YOU'RE O.K.
(Rainbows and Unicorns)

I'M O.K.
YOU'RE NOT O.K.
(Witch Hunt)

I'M NOT O.K. YOU'RE NOT O.K.
(We're Both Broken)

I'M NOT O.K.
YOU'RE O.K.
(Hero Worship)

"We" Zenith—1223 The Lateran Council of 1215 (eight years before the "We" Zenith of 1223) approved burning at the stake as a punishment against heresy, and the Synod of Toulouse confirmed this in 1229 (six years after that same "We" Zenith)

"We" Zenith—1543 Just eleven years past this "We" Zenith, England's "Bloody Mary" revived the practice of burning at the stake and offered 284 Protestants as her offering to God.

"We" Zenith—1703 The Salem Witch Trials of 1692 began just eleven years prior to this "We" Zenith. Irrational accusations followed by the death penalty were popular once again.

"We" Zenith—1783 This Zenith of "I'm OK, you're not OK" led to the introduction of the guillotine as the preferred method of execution during Robespierre's Reign of Terror in France (1793). Many of the twenty to forty thousand people he executed were not allowed to speak in their own defense at their trials.

"We" Zenith—1863 Self-righteous southerners faced off against self-righteous northerners in a horrifically bloody civil war between brothers (1861–1865).

CC Image courtesy of Mulica en Flickr

"We" Zenith—1943 Adolph Hitler was the German promoter of "I'm OK, you're not OK" (1933–1945). Joseph Stalin was the Soviet promoter during his "Great Purge" of 1936–1938. Senator Joseph McCarthy was the American witch-hunt specialist with the help of the "Un-American Activities Committee" from 1937 to 1953.

Figure 17.4 "WE" Zenith: Witch Hunts.

WE   WE ZENITHS

WE ALWAYS TAKE A GOOD THING TOO FAR

Witch hunts / Small actions—Zenith

1943	Adolph Hitler—The Holocaust
1936–1938	Joseph Stalin—Great Purge
1937–1953	Senator Joseph McCarthy—"Un-American Activities Committee"

Witch hunts / Small actions—Zenith

1863	American Civil War

Witch Hunts / Small Actions—Zenith

1783	Robespierre—Reign of Terror in France (1793)
1783	America wins Revolutionary War

Witch hunts / Small actions—Zenith

1703	Salem Witch Trials (1692)

Witch hunts / Small actions—Zenith

1543	"Bloody Mary" revived burning at the stake in 1554

Witch hunts / Small actions—Zenith

1223	Burning at the stake approved by Lateran Council of 1215

Keep in mind that this twenty-year season of "I'm OK, you're not OK" represents just one-fourth of the eighty-year round trip of a forty-year "Me" followed by a forty-year "We." This means the odds of a particular event randomly falling into this specific, twenty-year window are just one in four. Yet virtually every instance of widespread viciousness in Western society has happened within ten years of the Zenith of a "We."

2013–2033: **Who Will We Burn This Time?**

On the upside, the Zenith of a "We" offers some very specific marketing opportunities. Self-definition—"branding" if you will—is no longer determined by who you include and what you stand for; instead, it becomes a function of *ex*clusion: who you *ex*clude and what you stand *against*.

Here's the payoff: the easiest people in the world to manipulate are those who are focused on a single issue. Be forcefully *against* whatever they're against and you can lead them around like a tame calf on a rope. You can't have insiders without outsiders.

Figure 17.5   Upswing toward a "WE" Zenith.

Yes, marketing becomes very easy as we approach the Zenith of the "We." Just choose what and who you will demonize and then start tossing fear-soaked words as though they were longneck beer bottles full of gasoline with fiery rags stuffed down their throats. It's Machiavellian, we know, but it's true nonetheless. We wish we could bring you happier news, but the simple truth is this: unless we begin working together to soften this coming trend of "I'm OK, you're not OK," we're about to enter the ugliest twenty years of the Pendulum's eighty-year round trip.

To counteract the coming trend,

1. **Listen with your whole heart, and try not to interrupt.** Resist the temptation to put words into others' mouths. Don't be accusatory. Try to understand, truly, what "the other side" is saying. The last time we were in this "I'm OK, you're not OK" cycle, Ernest Hemingway is reported to have offered the perfect advice to his readers: "When people talk, listen completely. Most people never listen." It's time to heed that advice once again.

 Instantaneous worldwide communication might be able to help us mitigate the negativity and soften the viciousness of the next 20 years. But you must have the courage to speak up.
—*Michael R. Drew*

2. **Be capable of articulating calmly how "the other side" sees it.** Always acknowledge that goodness and sincerity can be found on both sides of every argument. Paul Hewitt said, "The person who can state his antagonist's point of view *to the satisfaction of the antagonist* is more likely to be correct than the person who cannot."[4] Most of us cannot articulate the position of our antagonist to the satisfaction of the antagonist because we fear that a clear understanding of their perspective might cause us to change our minds. And in an era of "I'm OK, you're not OK" this feels like the ultimate disaster because, if that were to happen, we would, by our own self-righteous definition, no longer be "OK."

When we discuss this Pendulum phenomenon with others, people often ask, "Will the advent of instantaneous worldwide communication (the Internet) accelerate the Pendulum?" The logic of this question is obvious, but we feel the answer is No.

If intellect or information drove the Pendulum, the answer would most certainly be Yes. But these things don't seem to drive the human heart. The pace of deep human change is agricultural—our motivations change at the speed of trees.

Think of a tree—a specific tree whose location you know. That tree seems not to change from day to day, right? And unless it's very young,

iStockphoto / nuno

it seems not even to change from year to year. But take a snapshot of that tree today and then come back in ten, twenty, or forty years, and it will be astoundingly different. This seems also to be the way of the human heart. Grief counselors are very familiar with this "agricultural" pace of the human heart, as it often takes a complete cycle of four seasons for an emotional wound to heal. When a member of one's immediate family is lost, a single cycle of four seasons barely begins this process of recovery. The Internet has done nothing to change this.

The good news, however, is that instantaneous worldwide communication might be able to help us mitigate the negativity and soften the viciousness of the next twenty years.

But you must have the courage to speak up.

Edmund Burke is reported to have said 240 years ago, "All that is necessary for the triumph of evil is that good men do nothing."

"A Catholic, a Mormon, a Jew, and an Evangelical sat down at a table together and . . . "

No, that wasn't the beginning of a joke. It's what happened on July 1, 2011, when four alumni of Wizard Academy decided to turn on a recorder before they began a discussion about the future. Two of the four were Roy H. Williams and Michael R. Drew, the authors of this book. They were joined by Tim Miles, a Wizard of Ads partner, and Jeffrey Eisenberg, who, with his brother Bryan Eisenberg, wrote the online marketing books *Waiting for Your Cat to Bark?* and *Call to Action.* Both books became *New York Times* and *Wall Street Journal* business best sellers.

This is a transcript of that discussion:

Roy: 2013 to 2023. Jeffrey, what do you think will happen?

Jeff: We're just sitting here and chatting, really, trying to understand the forces that you've shown us exist. But in the end most of us are very, very bad at knowing what will happen tomorrow, so when we try to predict what's going to happen in twenty, thirty, or forty years, we've got religious and secular orientations, and scientific orientations, and educational biases, and regional biases, and political biases. We have so many biases that get inserted into our predictions that I'm concerned the Pendulum reader will latch onto all the wrong predictions we're about to make and then use them to evaluate the quality of the basic idea. The "Me" and "We" forces are real and highly instructive, even if we can't use them to predict specific events.

Clockwise from top: Roy H. Williams (coauthor), Michael R. Drew (coauthor), Jeffery Eisenberg, Tim Miles.

Roy: That was very well said, Jeff.

Michael: I agree.

Roy: I have the same concerns about the reader disagreeing with our predictions and ignoring the truth of the Pendulum because of it, but in the end I decided that it would seem like a cop-out if we didn't end the book with at least our best guesses. Mike and I appreciate that you guys agreed to go out on a limb with us. Thanks, Jeffrey. Thanks, Tim.

Michael: Definitely. Thanks.

Tim: Maybe *one* prediction made by *one* of us will turn out to be correct. [Everyone laughs.]

Roy: So now that we've safely disclaimed everything we're about to say, what do you think will happen, Jeffrey? 2013 to 2023.

WE I believe we'll see a continuation of the trend to give up privacy for the greater good. We did it with the Patriot Act, and we did it again to get free stuff online and then along came Facebook. I believe we'll be pressured to give up our privacy in countless ways for the common and individual good. And in the end, we'll wind up with a tremendous loss of . . .

—*Jeffrey Eisenberg*

PhotoDune / Logoff

Roy: Are you talking about a continued invasion of privacy by the government, or will it be coming primarily from business?

Jeff: Most people don't yet realize that when they look something up on Google, it doesn't always show them what it might show someone else. A significant percentage of the search results from Google are personalized to the searcher based on what Google has learned about that person from their previous searches. This personalization of data just drives each of us deeper into a perceptual cocoon, right? And we are giving up privacy because we don't want to pay for stuff. We like the comfort of it. And there is also this feeling of needing to prove that we have nothing to hide.

Roy: I see.

Jeff: So there are a lot of different pressures for us to live publicly, right? Twitter is a public-feed thing. I mean, the pressures are increasingly to give up our privacy.

Tim: The fear I have is that it's becoming sort of a "villagers outside the gates with torches." There's a populist, almost excitement about battling any sort of resistance to the elimination of privacy, you know? If I want to celebrate privacy, well, "Then you must have something to hide . . ."

Jeff: Right.

Tim: And you're automatically guilty of something. I don't know what it is, but you're guilty, and I'm mad at you, and I'm going to tell everybody that you're doing something wrong."

Roy: Right. Now Michael. 2013 to 2023. What's your best speculation?

Michael: I think we are going to stay in a recession. We probably aren't going to see a full recovery of the economy until around 2023. I also think we are going to see, as Jeff was saying, a loss of privacy and a requirement to be completely open. I think we'll see better uses of social media for business. And I also think that the greatest capital we're going to have is our reputation. I know some kids, you know, teenagers, fifteen-, sixteen-year-olds, who are putting all their sexual exploits on Facebook because they think it's okay, you know? They don't understand that as they move forward that stuff is going to come back to bite them. Parents in today's culture just don't understand, yet the ramifications of being completely transparent and what it's going to mean to their children's lives as they go off to the university or as they apply for jobs and whatnot.

Roy: So, now, when parents begin to . . .

Jeff: Michael's right. This is probably the predominant trend we're going to see. All the rest of what we're going to say is going to be much more speculative. We've been watching this trend toward the voluntary loss of privacy, and this is clearly going to continue for another ten years.

Roy: Jeff, you, and Michael, and Tim might see this voluntary loss of privacy as a very self-evident thing, and I think you guys are probably correct, but that's not something I had really considered. What I think we can expect to see happen is that the general public will try to purge the system of corrupt politicians. We've seen too much self-serving among our politicians, and a "We" generation just won't stand for it. The recent Blagojevich conviction was the tip of the iceberg. And then came Anthony Weiner with his sexting scandal and then Newt Gingrich got a big surprise when he took the goodwill of the public and his campaign staff for granted. I believe in the second half of this Upswing into "We" we're going to elect political candidates who lift brooms during their speeches and promise, "I'm going to clean up Washington."

Jeff: I'm seeing the opposite. Andrew Sullivan has been writing, "So when did we become Rome? When did we go into decline?" Sullivan would say that what you're currently seeing is apathy, and his prediction is that this apathy will continue. I think I might agree with him.

iStockphoto / Jodi Jacobson

Roy: It'll be fun to see who is right.

Jeff: I don't think we'll see a political purge because, like Mike said, there's this transparency issue. You know, who doesn't live in a glass house? No one is going to be willing to cast the first stone. I think we can see evidence of this in Europe. Many of Europe's leaders are openly self-serving and hedonistic.

Tim: No, see, I hear . . .

Michael: I don't see it as a decline. In a "Me" it's all about the individual. We do things bigger and more verbose than who we really are. That translates into business and into government, and most of the politicians we're talking about were elected during a "Me." In a "We" culture, we start demanding authenticity and transparency in the marketplace.

Roy: I hear everything you've said, but I still disagree with it. Let me tell you why.

Jeff: That's why we're here, right? [laughs]

Roy: What you're calling apathy and what Andrew Sullivan is calling apathy is actually carefully disguised patience. I think we have a certain tolerance and patience, and then, when we finally reach the boiling point, we track down John Dillinger and Al Capone and "Pretty Boy" Floyd and Bonnie and Clyde, and we lock 'em up, and the hero is the FBI.

Jeff: So, but you're talking about from 2013 . . .

Roy: 2013 to 2023, right.

Jeff: . . . to 2023. I don't think it can happen that fast. And I don't feel comfortable in saying that what Andrew Sullivan is talking about is apathy. I think that what he's saying is that we are in decline.

National Union of Journalists

George Orwell

Roy: Now here's the thing. I *violently* disagree with Andrew Sullivan and his comparison of our current condition to the decline of Rome, and I think Michael agrees with me, but . . . yes, Michael's nodding his head . . .

Michael: Mm-hmm.

Roy: Go back exactly eighty years, when the Pendulum was in the same position and headed in the same direction as it is now. You'd be in 1932, and we were passing all kinds of laws prohibiting the sale of alcohol and restricting other freedoms, and it wouldn't be many more years until we were locking up all the Japanese Americans in our own version of concentration camps. America never talks about these Japanese internment camps because we're ashamed of what we did. But any time the government begins to feel empowered by the people to invade privacy and impose restrictions on the population "for the common good" we're going to do these sorts of things.

So let's summarize. I think the one thing we all agreed on was that we'll likely continue to give up our privacy. Big Brother is alive and well, and George Orwell was right.

Jeff: Right, except that instead of the government watching us as Orwell predicted, we're actually just watching each other.

Michael: Well, see, I think it's a combination of Orwell's *1984* and Aldous Huxley's *Brave New World,* which was written exactly eighty years ago. I think it's a combination of both, not just *1984*.

Aldous Huxley

Roy: When did Orwell write *1984*?

Michael: 1948, published in '49.

Jeff: Oh, stop talking about all the *GAMMAS* that you live around.[5]

Michael: [laughs]

Roy: If we say that we've given up liberties in exchange for the perception of security and that this is going to continue to be a trend . . .

Jeff: And not just security. It's also the public desire for "free." We've become funnily frugal about things . . .

Tim: So you mean financially "free." You're not talking about liberty . . .

Jeff: . . . Yes, yes, yes, that's what I'm saying. We don't seem to value intellectual property in the same way that a "Me" cycle would. We feel that when intellectual property is beneficial, "Well, why can't I reproduce it? Why can't I mash it up? It's enjoyable, I get benefit out of it." So we've given up on this idea of personal authorship, not yet in a fully financial sense, but to a great degree infringements that we consider acceptable today would not have been considered acceptable twenty years ago.

2023–2043

Roy: Okay, let's talk about 2023 to 2043, the Downswing of the "We," when this all starts losing some of its energy. We've been doing good for so long that people get swept forward by the momentum of it until it becomes societal obligation and we get worried about social appearances.

Tim: My children are going to have me killed

ALL: [laughter]

Tim: 'cause I'll be in their way, old and slow.

Joseph McCarthy

CC Image

Roy: Tim, that's kind of what happened in the Downswing of the last "We." Joseph McCarthy came to power and started pointing his finger at people he suspected of being communists. You had the blacklists. Lives were ruined. Everyone was paranoid and afraid . . .

Tim: So Glenn Beck was just fifteen years too early!

ALL: [laughter]

Michael: 2023 to 2030. I think the United States will continue to move toward globalization. We've lost the Industrial Revolution. That's moved to China. That's moved to India. If we want to look at competing internationally, we're going to have to do it by being ahead of the rest of the world in terms of education and in terms of opportunity, and I think that what we'll be doing is changing our educational system so that we're able to develop more entrepreneurs. . . .

Jeff: You think that ten, thirty years from now we'll still have an advantage in education?

Michael: I think we currently have an opportunity advantage when it comes to education. It's more readily available in the United States than in most countries. We're certainly not number one in education right now, but we do have an opportunity advantage. But when India and China have enough money coming in twenty years of working in the mill or at the factory, they'll start to raise children who will have at least as much opportunity as we enjoy in the West . . .

Jeff: I'm going to disagree because I think what you're explaining has something with a nationalist tinge, and what we wind up with is . . .

Roy: Hang on a sec! We're off topic. Stay focused on what you think will happen in Western society from 2023 to 2043.

Jeff: I believe we'll have much more of a caste system than we've ever seen before. Society will be divided into knowledge workers, industrial workers, and agricultural workers. There will be cities like Austin, New York, and Portland, where knowledge workers live, and those people will have stronger relationships with the knowledge workers in Mumbai than they'll have with the agricultural workers who live just twenty miles away. I think we're going to see more and more of this caste system because what it takes to stay ahead is a level of education and indoctrination to values that are becoming more and more difficult to penetrate. In the United States, we already have a less porous social class system than we've ever had before, and it's starting to happen all over the world. To enter the "knowledge worker" class is becoming more difficult to accomplish if you weren't born into it.

Roy: Alright, here's what I want you guys to do. Think of a single sentence to encapsulate what you think will happen. Summarize it as sharply as you can. 2023 to 2043. Tim, what are you thinking?

Tim: I think we're going to see a continuing erosion of public education.

Roy: Why?

 The new debate in education will be about how to create new pathways to wealth. The old path doesn't go there anymore.
—*Michael R. Drew*

Tim: Kids haven't had anyone nipping at their heels or any sort of challenges or worries about what might happen to them. They no longer buy into the idea that they need a college degree. I believe society is headed back to the old Renaissance idea of scholars. Scholars congregate at universities. Learned thinkers are at universities. Someone who's going to be a knowledge worker doesn't necessarily need a university degree anymore. They just need training. Being a knowledge worker is more of a trade, but these new trades aren't industrial anymore. They're technologically and intellectually based. I think we're going to see a sort of divisiveness in education that will cause a lot of new problems and challenges.

Jeff: You see a greater distinction of the class system?

Tim: Yes.

Roy: Jeff, summarize your thoughts.

Jeff: I believe there will be a backlash against organizers of religion whose message revolves around money, okay? And political power. There will be a backlash. I also believe the West is becoming postnationalist, and a worker-class system will develop because instantaneous, worldwide communication is everywhere and it's free. Classism will develop because we'll relate to workers in our own class in other countries more than we relate to workers in a different class in our own country.

Roy: Michael, summarize your thoughts.

Michael: I think we're going to see what Tim and Jeffrey both said. I foresee a massive debate regarding the future of education, and it will be related to the creation of wealth. Specifically, how do we maintain our middle class? If you look back at what came out of the last "We," it was infrastructure. We had industry, and wealth was built by workers going out, getting jobs, being paid more and more for their work, creating pensions and buying into the system, going to college, getting a job, staying with the company. . . .

iStockphoto / scibak

INDIA

Jeff: Are you saying that's what you think will happen?

Michael: No, I said that's what happened back *then*. The new debate in education will be about how to create new pathways to wealth. The old path doesn't go there anymore.

Jeff: People with wealth relate to other people with wealth no matter where they might live. Our current globalization is the globalization of a caste system that results in an erosion of national interests. American manufacturers no longer struggle to manufacture their products in the United States. They're no longer worried about employing Americans. They just want to make money. American companies are just as happy to create jobs in China and India. Money recognizes no borders between nations.

CHINA

iStockphoto / hronos7

Roy: I think you're going to see a *huge* resurgence of labor unions as the middle class continues to get squeezed. "Working together for the common good" is the driving force in a "We," and labor unions are a natural expression of it. I'm not pro-union, but I believe labor unions are going to gain momentum near the Zenith of the "We" whether I'm in favor of them or not.

Jeff: I hate to sound Marxist, but workers of the world will unite. We're seeing the gutting of the middle class. We can no longer expect to live like our parents did. They could live really nicely on one salary while the other parent stayed home and took care of the kids. We no longer have that expectation, and we've continued to lower our expectations for the past several years.

Tim: I don't disagree with you regarding how money flows across borders, but I think most people will remain uninformed. People tend to look at problems superficially, never really grappling with the primary cause.

PhotoDune / lucadp

Jeff: We've had safety valves and all sorts of things that are slowly disappearing. You know, those safety valves that are quickly letting off the steam?

Roy: What you're saying, Jeffrey, is that they have not yet had to eliminate Social Security.

Jeff: Correct! And the thing is, they will never eliminate social security. I believe they will inflate it.

Michael: I disagree with that. I think that for the last thirty years, for most of my life, we've been talking about the insolvency of social security. I don't think the ones who are going to see it cut have a full expectation of it being there anyway.

Jeff: But you know what? They also don't expect old people to be dying in the streets. I'm not saying that's going to happen, but we've seen inflation in the Carter years, okay, and we're going to need a minimum of that kind of inflation to inflate our way out of our problems and the cost of living. . . .

Roy: Now Jeffrey, you said something very interesting. You said "we've" seen. You and I remember the Jimmy Carter years, but do Michael and Tim? Michael said "in my thirty years." So we have a thirty-year-old Mormon, a forty-five-year-old Jew, a fifty-three-year-old Evangelical Christian and . . . ?

Tim: A forty-year-old-year-old Catholic.

Roy: . . . and a forty-year-old-year-old Catholic. [Everyone laughs.] That's kind of interesting.

Tim: Is it possible that one of the Alpha Voices in our future will have something to do with, I dunno, a group who gets together and cracks cold fusion, and the game changes, and suddenly the idea of oil for energy that we've been burdened with for, you know, since the Industrial Revolution, changes the game, changes the rules. Is that a possibility?

Jeff: [Speaking to Tim] You and I have had this discussion. We've talked about it on the phone. So if cold fusion happened, we walk away from carbon-based energy into a better form of energy. And the way the world looks at things, scientific discovery, a lot of things would change.

2043–2063

Roy: Guys, this is that part of the discussion when I want you to go out onto the skinny part of the branch. Let's talk about the Upswing of the next "Me." 2043 to 2063. Think that far ahead. 2043 to 2063.

Jeff: Well, it's interesting. I believe the Alpha Voices of 2033 will be heroic in that they take themselves off the grid. They'll refuse the implants that we put into ourselves to stay on the grid. You know, communications and things. The Alpha Voices will be people who say, "No, I'm an individual, I'm me. . . ."

Michael: It's a Philip Dick and Margaret Atwood kind of thing coming to fruition. These Alpha Voice heroes, living in a world where science fiction starts to become real life. . . .

PhotoDune / scythers

Jeff: Well, I mean the logical thing is that we'll have implants, cognitively. William Gibson says that the future is just not widely distributed today. We could implant phones . . .

Roy: He said what? The future . . .

Jeff: The future is not widely distributed or something to that effect. It's worth looking up.

Roy: And who said it?

Jeff: William Gibson.

Roy: William Gibson.[6]

Jeff: I believe that within the next forty years we'll be living with implants, bioengineered with mechanically engineered enhancements.

Tim: Well, then why couldn't we live to be a hundred and twenty?

Jeff: I mean, we could.

Michael: I agree with you about the implants and about how the Alpha Voices will refuse them as we approach the beginning of the next "Me." Have you guys heard of augmented reality [AR]?

Tim: Like when you point a smart phone in GPS mode at something and an additional graphic appears onscreen on top of the thing you're looking at?

Michael: Exactly. Augmented reality combines virtual reality with actual reality. I believe the Alpha Voices of 2033 to 2043 will reject these implants because they'll represent the complete loss of personal identity and privacy.

Roy: Slow down. You lost me.

Michael: If we use the analogy of cooking a live frog by slowly heating up the water until the frog is dead, augmented reality is part of what's going to "heat up" the water so that our society relaxes its anxiety toward accepting implants. I believe it's this augmented reality technology, coupled with RFID Tags and streaming social media at its most extreme, that will lead to the acceptance of implants.

Roy: You know who you sound like, don't you?

Michael: [sigh] Tell me.

Roy: You're Sarah Connor and this augmented reality thing is Skynet.

[Everyone laughs]

Jeffrey: *Terminator?*

Roy: Skynet was the early artificial intelligence [AI] software program that evolved and took over humanity.

Tim: Here's what Google says about augmented reality: "Augmentation is conventionally in real-time and in semantic context with environmental elements, such as sports scores on TV during a match. With the help of advanced AR technology the information about the surrounding real world of the user becomes interactive and digitally manipulable. Artificial information about the environment and its objects can be overlaid on the real world . . . [As an example] the yellow 'first down' line seen in television broadcasts of American football games shows the line the offensive team must cross to receive a first down."

Roy: 2043 to 2063. I'm going to say this only briefly, but I think it's funny that it came up just after I pointed out our different backgrounds. Considering the different perspectives and training that are given to Evangelicals, Mormons, Catholics, and Jews, it's really funny that it would be the Jewish guy rather than the Evangelical who would propose an idea that has long been taught in Evangelical churches. Implants. The Book of Revelation. The mark of the beast. Evangelicals have always been fascinated with a passage in Revelation 13 that says the people in the last days can "neither buy nor sell" without the mark of the beast. The speculation for the last fifty years is that this mark would obviously have to be something that replaces money, an implanted chip of some kind, so that your hand would be scanned during a financial transaction. Robbery, credit card theft, and identity theft will be eliminated because the physical person is required to effect every transaction. Jeffrey, you have no idea how much you sounded like an Evangelical Christian evangelist just then. You have absolutely no idea.

Jeff: And I don't even play one on television! [Everyone laughs.] I like science fiction, but I dislike prediction. I'm not crazy about what we're doing. It's a nice conversation, but, you know, it's pure speculation.

Roy: It's absolute speculation. But it's impossible to write about the Pendulum of society without speculating about what might happen next. Michael and I really appreciate you and Tim sharing your thoughts.

Jeff: This idea, my central idea, which is this loss of privacy, is about us giving up increasing amounts of privacy for convenience, for power, for payments, for conformity. If I was to think of this as a Book of Revelation thing, then yes, we'd have to include the rise of a Christ-like hero, but I'm actually not saying that.

What I'm saying is that some Alpha Voices will be real heroes and take themselves off the grid.

Roy: When you talk about taking yourself off the grid and suffering the consequences of it, you're sort of describing Keanu Reeves when he is awakened in the *Matrix*. When he decides to step out of the dream that is the matrix. . . .

Jeff: Yeah, he took the red pill.

Roy: . . . and now all of a sudden it's a pretty gritty existence, but at least he has his purity or whatever. . . . Now Michael, 2043 to 2063. What happens?

Michael: One of two things is going to happen: Either from 2023 to 2043 we're going to work out something economically and be back in a time frame when most of the workers will have been the worker bees for twenty-plus years, and their kids will start to reject that type of conformity in 2043, or we're going to be in a position where we've gone into a massive decline, a decades-long recession from which we haven't been able to recover economically, and we're going to be looking for economic leaders who will . . .

Jeff: You keep using the word recession as if it has meaning. Again, we're talking about a future thing and part of this, we've just gone back, we just started talking about the "Me," but in the "We," which we're firmly in right now, there's a real rejection at a fundamental level of a national recession. We're in Austin, Texas, where the effects of the recession are negligible. And there are other places in the world where you'd hardly know it, and yet, we could drive less than five hours and see places that look like they're in a depression. I think that's part of the point that you're missing. So when you're talking about economies recovering, the question becomes economies recovering for whom?

Michael: For the masses, the majority, there's New York, San Francisco . . .

Roy: And so in this "Me" of 2043 to 2063, Michael, what happens?

Michael: This is why I'm raising the question, because it partially depends on where we end up economically at that point. If we've come up with an economic solution, there will be one response. If we haven't, then I believe that the "Me" cycle will actually produce concepts and ideas that will help pull us out of economic crisis, whether you want to call it a recession, or . . .

Jeff: I see them as revolutionaries. The "Mes" will wind up looking much more like revolutionaries. We've got this whole "We" cycle to work through this group thing, this forming of classes, and I think that in 2043 what we're looking at is a much more revolutionary-type cycle where people start talking about empowering themselves as individuals.

Michael: I agree, but my question is whether that's going to be from an economic standpoint due to the masses being in a lower class system that wants to break through, or is it going to come from a more spiritual, individualistic standpoint, a breaking away from technology?

Jeff: Are these things necessarily different?

Roy: Tim, 2043 to 2063. What do you think? What happens?

ME First, I don't want my children to eat me as food. Second, I want a ray gun. [Everyone laughs.] Seriously, though, my son will be my age, and he'll have grown up with computer chips, and they won't be fascinating to him like they are to us. I think there's a real possibility for the next "Me" to be an age of

enlightenment. People will be so confident in the tools they have that their basic need to spread their wings and explore could easily usher in a time of really extraordinary advances.

—*Tim Miles*

Jeff: I can buy into that. You just described a future for the knowledge-worker class, which is a step below, or maybe a couple of steps below the top line—wealthy people.

Figure 17.6 What's coming next?

WE	A LOOK AHEAD: A PREDICTION OF EVENTS IN 2013–2063

2013 to 2023: In the second half of a "We" Upswing and the first half of the Downswing — essentially.

2023–2033: We become more oriented to the self-righteous perspective, "I'm OK, You're not OK." This opens the door for deeply entrenched ideologues who are all mouth and no ears, hard-fisted leaders who expect to be heard but who never listen — Joseph McCarthy, Joseph Stalin, Adolph Hitler. These leaders create insular groups who believe everyone else is wrong. The popular thing will be to assign blame. It is a time of finger pointing—not a pretty picture socially. Frankly, my plan is not to be among the majority. I plan to live completely counter to this trend.

My primary reason for agreeing to publish *Pendulum* is the rather optimistic hope that it will cause some people to think twice and resist this inevitable trend toward blame shifting and fear.

2033–2043: Partly due to the rise of ideologues, the Downswing of a "We" is when much is done just for the sake of appearances. Conformity will be expected. Outliers will be scorned. The Alpha Voices in technology and literature will be heard in 2033, and my best guess about the new musical genre of 2038 can only be described as a crossword puzzle of statements spoken in rhythm.

Michael: If you have a class system that basically puts 75 percent of the world in poverty, I think that . . .

Jeff: Poverty is relevant, so let's differentiate between people dying in the streets of hunger and people having the basic necessities. Forty years ago we imagined the middle class being a vastly different thing than it is today, and forty years from now we'll imagine the middle class as being, "Hey, they eat, they go to school, they can get jobs, they have transportation." You know, pretty basic stuff.

Roy: A few minutes ago I mentioned that any book about the Pendulum of society would need to end with some speculation about what might happen next. I've played the role of moderator so far and let you guys go out on the limb without me, and that's not fair. So here are my best guesses about what is likely to happen.

Tim: What do you mean?

Roy: You've heard "row, row, row your boat" sung in rounds, right?

Tim: Sure.

Roy: Imagine a group of performers, each reciting their own poem simultaneously. You can focus on just one voice and follow that story, or you can focus on an entirely different voice telling a different story, or, due to the interplay of cadence, rhythm, and meter, you can hear a series of completely different messages by listening "across" the performers. In other words, you might listen to three words from the first performer, then catch the next couple of words from a different performer, then switch to a third performer to complete the sentence. A virtually infinite number of phrases, encouragements, reprimands, and slogans could be woven into a song using this technique. If we compare rap to playing chess on a single chessboard, this new musical genre would be

iStockphoto / Burwell Photography

like chess played on three chessboards stacked vertically with every piece free to be moved at will to its appropriate position on either of the other two chessboards.

Tim: I need a hit of whatever you're smoking. [Everyone laughs.]

Roy: And then when we hit the Zenith of 2063, everyone will start wearing big hair again, and photographers will use backlighting so the hair always seems to glow heroically. [Everyone laughs.]

Tim: Just like in Jeffrey's high school yearbook photo?

Jeff: Hey! [Everyone laughs.]

Roy: 2043 to 2063. As we begin our next "Me," China and India will have just finished their own forty-year "Me," the result of which will be that land in Canada and in Mongolia at about fifty-three degrees north latitude will be extremely expensive because everyone will be trying to move there.

Jeff: Global warming?

Roy: Bingo. China currently has nearly thirty thousand miles of limited access freeway. This is almost triple what they had in 2001. The United States, by comparison, has only forty-seven thousand miles of interstate. China is expected to surpass that number by 2020 and will shortly thereafter be consuming more gasoline than America and Europe combined. You might convince people in a "We" to reduce their consumption of fossil fuels, but China is currently in a "Me" that won't end until 2043, when birds are bursting into flames in midair.

Michael: What do you say when someone says that science has not yet proven a link between fossil fuels and global warming?

Roy: When I was a kid, the big argument was that science had never proven a link between cigarette smoking and cancer. But most of the people who were making that argument died from emphysema, so you don't hear it much anymore. Does anybody have any last words that they'd like to add?

Michael: I'd like to go back to our conversation about class and where we're headed.

Jeff: You're fun, Mike. Classism is like climate change. It's happening, and it's either recognized or it's not, right?

Michael: But I think there's still time to make changes within our culture.

Jeff: Now turn off that recorder and I'll tell you what I'd never want to go on record as having said.

Roy: Okay . . . [Click]

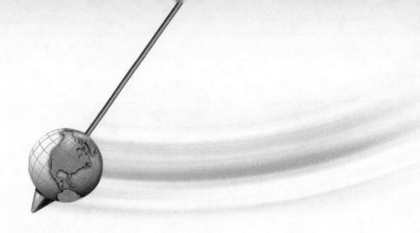

Pendulum Legend

Sales and promotional techniques that were effective in the United States in 1972 will be equally effective in China and India in 2012 . . . You'll be hailed as a marketing genius. Or maybe our theory is wrong, and you'll look like an idiot. You decide.

CHAPTER EIGHTEEN

Uses of the Pendulum

In an Upswing of "Me," we quote Henry David Thoreau, that great individualist of *Walden* who said, "If a man does not keep pace with his companions, perhaps it is because he hears a different drummer. Let him step to the music which he hears, however measured or far away."

We think, *Oh, yes. It's so meaningful! I will march to the beat of a different drummer. I will be my own person. I'm unique. I'm special. And by all that is holy, L'Oréal is right. I'm worth it! I have value. I'm a winner.*

Motivational speakers get wealthy during a "Me." Do you remember the popularity of positive thinking in the 1980s? The fact that yesterday's "You can do it! You're a winner!" crowd is currently making a fortune in China is just one more indication that Eastern culture swings "Me" when Western culture is swinging "We."

Gandhi, that selfless leader who united the people of India for the common good, was also inspired by Henry David Thoreau, but in a different way and from a different writing. Speaking of Thoreau, Gandhi said, "He taught nothing he was not prepared to practice in himself. He was one of the greatest

CC Image

and most moral men America has produced. At the time of the abolition of slavery movement, he wrote his famous essay, 'On the Duty of Civil Disobedience.' He went to jail for the sake of his principles and suffering humanity. His essay has, therefore, been sanctified by suffering."

It is, of course, no coincidence that Thoreau wrote his famous essay in 1849, during the seventh year of an Upswing in a Western "We."

It's common to see suffering as a virtue when we've passed the Zenith of a "We," but Gandhi made his "suffering is good" statement in 1907, very near the Zenith of the Western "Me" of 1903. This is another subtle indication that the Pendulum of the East hits the Zenith of "We" just as the West hits the Zenith of "Me." Gandhi, in the Eastern "We" of 1903, was inspired by Thoreau's civil disobedience and took it to a whole new level.

The next Eastern Zenith of "We" was 1983. Their "Me" Zenith will be 2023. We expect 2023 in Asia to look very much like 1983 looked in America.

So if China and India are swinging "Me" while Western society is swinging "We," might there be a practical, productive, profitable use for this information?

Of course there is. If you want to sell products or services in China or India, study the techniques that were effective in the United States exactly forty years ago. Forty-year-old magazines, books, and newspapers will be your best sources of inspiration. Sales and promotional techniques that were effective in the United States in 1972 will be similarly effective in China and India in 2012. Just make the necessary adjustments for language and culture, then reintroduce your historically proven technique. You'll be hailed as a marketing genius.

Or maybe our theory is wrong, and you'll look like an idiot. You decide.

Let's talk a bit more about marketing.

Ernest Dichter (1907–1991) was an American psychologist and the marketing expert who is considered to be the father of motivational research. In the December 1966 issue of *Harvard Business Review*[1], Dichter identified the four basic motivators that drive consumers to talk about their experiences with products and product messages.

1. **Product-involvement.** The experience is so novel and pleasurable that it must be shared. Dichter estimated that product involvement drives one-third of all discussions about products.

2. **Self-involvement.** This is a way to gain attention, demonstrate connoisseurship, identify oneself as having insider status, or assert superiority over others. Dichter estimated that self-involvement drives nearly a quarter of all discussions.

Keep in mind that Dichter conducted this study in 1966, during the Upswing of a "Me."

3. **Other-involvement.** This is a desire to express neighborliness, caring, and friendship. In a "Me," other-involvement drives less than one-fifth of purchases.

4. **Message-involvement.** The information is so humorous or informative that it cries out to be shared. Again, in a "Me," message-involvement drives slightly less than one-fifth of purchases.

We can easily conclude from Dichter's study that product-involvement and self-involvement would be the keys to selling in India and China, as they seem to be currently swinging toward "Me."

But two questions remain.

1. Does other-involvement gain importance during a "We"? Should American marketers get involved with saving the environment and other social issues? Successful ad campaigns of recent years would lead us to believe this answer to be Yes.
2. Does message-involvement gain importance in a "We"? Should American marketers invest in messages that are notable for their humor and perspective? The success of Facebook and Twitter would seem to indicate this answer to be Yes as well.

Here's what marketing looks like during a "We": a woman is shopping with her boyfriend for engagement rings in one of the ten thousand–square-foot showrooms of Spence Diamonds. She steps into the ladies room, where she finds the following message on the wall. It's an example of "other-involvement" as described by Ernest Dichter.

WE So this is it. Wow. You're about to choose the ring you'll wear forever. And that guy out there is The One. Not exactly how you used to imagine him, is he? Don't let it bother you. Men have been falling short of women's expectations for centuries. But somehow it all works out. The secret is to look past all his outward bravado and awkwardness to see the boy he is inside. Seriously. Little girls grow up and become adults. Boys, well, they just get taller. You know, it's not too late to go out there, look him in the eye, and say, "I've changed my mind." Life without him would be a lot less complicated, that's for sure. The house would stay cleaner, the bills would be smaller, and you wouldn't have to be forgiving him constantly for all those idiotic things men do. Maybe you could get a cat. I've heard cats make good companions. But then, however, he does make you laugh. Cats don't do that. And you know he'd jump in front of a train to save you. He sees something magical in you. That's why he's out there, right now, waiting. Feels good, doesn't it? So what's it going to be—a cleaner house or a life of adventure? If you choose the adventure, go out that door and surprise him with a kiss. Don't tell him what it's for. Let it be just another small part of the wonderful mystery that is you.

Did you notice that this message on the stall of the ladies bathroom in Spence Diamonds contains *no* information about the company or its products? This strange piece of writing illustrates the difference between *pulling* people into a relationship through positive attraction as opposed to *pushing* them into a decision through a "needs analysis" and then "overcoming their objections."

Pull works better than push during a "We," even when you're writing ads for classic mass media like signage, television, radio, and newspaper.

The "push" strategy of direct marketing did exceptionally well during the last "Me," but the old gurus of direct marketing saw their businesses fall apart at the end of the 2003–2008 transitionary window into the current "We."

ME = Push
WE = Pull

2003–2043 will be a "We" for all of Western society.

People assume the Internet and social media are driving today's society. The truth, however, is quite the opposite: it is our "We" society that is driving both the Internet and social media.

WE The Internet is not a sales or marketing tool; rather, it is a relationship-building device.

—Michael R. Drew

Online relationships are built through conversation, just as they have always been built offline.

The Internet is a "pull" medium, serving up only what is requested.

Successful online marketing is based on creating an appropriate response to the actions or inquiries of the customer. It is barely conceivable in the online world that a marketing strategy might be crafted to "push" a customer into taking action. Yet a large number of marketers are still trying to use yesterday's "push" tactics online.

Good luck with that.

A dynamic "Me" personality believes in "overcoming objections." Selling is combat—push.

A responsive "We" personality believes in "positive attraction." Selling is seduction—pull.

Business Insider tells us that 96 percent of Americans use Facebook, and *Edison Research* adds that forty-six million of us check our social media profiles daily. Do you have a place in social media? Remember: it's not about marketing, it's about conversation and relationship. Don't pound your visitors; instead, seduce them into spending time with you. Whoever wins their time is the one most likely to win their money.

The slogans of McDonald's, the most successful franchise in the history of marketing, reflect an uncanny sensitivity to the mood of the public.

Figure 18.1 Popular slogans are a reflection of the current cycle.

WE	MCDONALD'S SLOGANS (1960–2008)	ME

1960: All American Menu: A Hamburger, Fries, and a Shake

1961: Look for the Golden Arches

1962: Go for the Goodness at McDonald's

1963: (The year 1963 is the tipping point into "Me." Early adopters are embracing the perspective, but the six-year transitionary window is only just beginning.)

1965: McDonald's: Where Quality Starts Fresh Every day

1966: McDonald's: The Closest Thing to Home

(Notice what happens as we approach the end of the six-year transitionary window into "Me" and ride the Pendulum to its Zenith of 1983 [(emphasis added].)

1967: McDonald's Is *Your* Kind of Place / It's Such a Happy Place

1971: *You* Deserve a Break Today

1975: We Do It All for *You*

1976: *You, You're* the One

1981: *You* Deserve a Break Today (reintroduction)

1983: McDonald's and *You* (continues to 1991)

(Now that we're eight years beyond the Zenith of "Me" and our self-obsession has begun to diminish a bit, let's see what happens next . . . .)

1991: Food, Folks and Fun

1995: Have You Had Your Break Today?

1997: Did Somebody Say McDonald's?

2000: *We* Love to See You Smile

2002: There's a Little McDonald's in Everyone

2003: I'm Lovin' It

(This is the end of the "Me." Look below at what happened in 2008, the final year of the six-year transition into "We.")

2008: What *We're* Made Of

Figure 18.2   Characteristics of effective sales methods in a "ME" cycle versus those in a "WE" cycle.

WE	VERSUS	ME
	SELLING/ MARKETING IN A "ME" VERSUS A "WE"	
"CUT THE CRAP AND GIVE IT TO ME STRAIGHT."		"YOU'RE SELLIN' HOPE, AND I'M BUYIN' IT LIKE IT'S CRACK COCAINE."
• Pull		• Push
• Positive Attraction		• Overcoming Objections
• Selling is Seduction		• Selling is Combat
• Authenticity		• Self Confidence and Belief
• Reality and Truth		• Advertising Specials
• Steak		• Sizzle

Do these things and your business will soar.

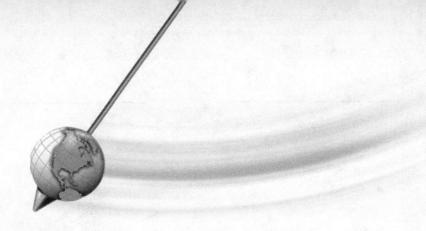

Pendulum Legend

Do we, in fact, become a different people
every forty years?

CHAPTER NINETEEN

Pendulum in the Bible

Moses was forty years old when he tried to lead Israel out of Egypt with the strength of his own arm. He failed in this effort, then ran like a little girl from the anger of Pharaoh. But who can blame him for trying? He was, after all, the only Israelite who had been raised in the palace under the protection of Pharaoh's daughter. "I'm unique. I'm special. I was born for this," he thought. Moses at forty was fully "Me"—brash, confident, full of himself. He was the kind of leader who would stand on the deck of an aircraft carrier, look into the lens of a TV camera, and say, "Mission accomplished."

But Moses at eighty was a completely different man. In the book of Numbers, we read, "Now the man Moses was very meek, the most humble man on the face of the whole earth."[1] Having lived his second forty years as a shepherd on the backside of the desert, Moses had lost his hubris and developed a speech impediment.

Remember the number of years the unbelieving Israelites had to wander in the desert before they became a completely different people? Bingo—forty years.

That phrase "forty years" appears fifty-four times in the Bible, and in virtually every instance it refers to an epoch, a window of transformative change.

Do we, in fact, become a different people every forty years?

Here are a few of those Biblical references to forty years:

WE When Moses was forty years old, he decided to visit his fellow Israelites. [Moses tries to lead Israel and fails, then runs into the desert.]

—Acts 7:23

After forty years had passed, an angel appeared to Moses in the flames of a burning bush in the desert near Mount Sinai [Moses is now eighty.]

—Acts 7:30

ME Then Moses went out and spoke these words to all Israel: I am now 120 years old, and I am no longer able to lead you. The LORD has said to me, "You shall not cross the Jordan." [Moses at the entrance to the Promised Land after wandering forty years in the wilderness.]

—Deuteronomy 31:2

So the land had peace for forty years, until Othniel son of Kenaz [Caleb's younger brother] died.

—Judges 3:11

So may all your enemies perish, O LORD! But may they who love you be like the sun when it rises in its strength." Then the land had peace forty years. [The ending of the *Song of Deborah*]

—Judges 5:31

Thus Midian was subdued before the Israelites and did not raise its head again. During Gideon's lifetime, the land enjoyed peace forty years. [Gideon's death]

—Judges 8:28

Again the Israelites did evil in the eyes of the LORD, so the LORD delivered them into the hands of the Philistines for forty years. [The birth of Samson]

—Judges 13:1

When he mentioned the ark of God, Eli fell backward off his chair by the side of the gate. His neck was broken and he died, for he was an old man and heavy. He had led Israel forty years.

—1 Samuel 4:18

David was thirty years old when he became king, and he reigned forty years.

—2 Samuel 5:4

Solomon reigned in Jerusalem over all Israel forty years.

—1 Kings 11:42

Joash was seven years old when he became king, and he reigned in Jerusalem forty years. His mother's name was Zibiah; she was from Beersheba. [Joash repairs the Temple]

—2 Chronicles 24:1

I will make the land of Egypt a ruin and a desolate waste from Migdol to Aswan, as far as the border of Cush. The foot of neither man nor beast will pass through it; no one will live there for forty years. I will make the land of Egypt desolate among devastated lands, and her cities will lie desolate forty years among ruined cities. And I will disperse the Egyptians among the nations and scatter them through the countries. Yet this is what the Sovereign LORD says: "At the end of forty years I will gather the Egyptians from the nations where they were scattered. I will bring them back from captivity and return them to Upper Egypt, the land of their ancestry. There they will be a lowly kingdom. It will be the lowliest of kingdoms and will never again exalt itself above the other nations. I will make it so weak that it will never again rule over the nations."

—Ezekiel 29:10–15

Note: It has been suggested to us that perhaps *forty years* was merely an ancient Hebrew expression that meant "a very long time" and didn't actually refer to a literal number of years. But even if this is the case, it seems reasonable that the number *forty* was chosen because the ancient Hebrews had noticed how reliably things became totally different during that span of years. Consequently, the phrase came to mean, "a long window of time during which things become totally different." But this is semantic hair splitting and we promised not to do that. Sorry.

William Strauss and Neil Howe didn't mention the Bible in *Generations* but focused instead on the historical record of Western society from 1584 to the present, a deeply detailed study of more than four hundred years. Not bad. Now let's overlay the twenty-year "generations" of Strauss and Howe onto the story of Moses. Our goal is to illustrate how these four strokes of the Pendulum follow a natural progression. The motivations and decisions of Moses demonstrate perfectly the principles of "Me" and "We."

1. *Idealist, marked by infatuation:* The Zenith of the "Me," this is symbolized by Moses at forty, full of himself, thinking, *I'm special.*

2. *Reactive, marked by disillusionment:* The Downswing of the "Me" to the fulcrum, this is symbolized by Moses at sixty after twenty years in the desert: "I'm searching for something better."

3. *Civic, marked by a power struggle:* The Upswing of the "We" to the Zenith, this is symbolized by Moses at eighty—"just a regular guy trying to make it through the day"—who encounters a burning bush and becomes aware of a problem that needs to be corrected. He then found himself facing off with Pharaoh in a power struggle over the future of the children of Israel.

4. *Adaptive, marked by reluctant acceptance:* The Downswing of the "We" to the fulcrum, this is symbolized by Moses at one hundred, leading Israel in the wilderness: "I'm part of a team on a journey."

When the four strokes of the Pendulum have completed their eighty-year journey, the society returns to the point where it began and the journey is begun anew:

ME *Idealist,* marked by infatuation, this is the Upswing of the "Me" to the fulcrum once again and is symbolized by Moses at 120, full of himself once more, striking the rock to bring water instead of speaking to the rock as God instructed: "I'm special."

As we mentioned earlier, the Pendulum can't be used to predict events involving individuals; however, the Pendulum becomes readily apparent when we begin looking at the broader strokes of the brush—the bigger picture of a society over time.

The religious thoughts of a society often reflect the position of the Pendulum as we ascribe to God the "good" characteristics that we believe to be self-evident. Most of us believe in a God whose opinions reflect our own. Perhaps Spencer Marsh said it best in his book, *God, Man and Archie Bunker*: "In the beginning, Archie created God in his own image. In his own image created he him."[2] Richard Exley, a minister, compared the freewheeling "Me" interpretation of the Bible to the authoritative "We" interpretation agreed upon by a group and reflected,

> Upon first reading I found his statement clever and attention grabbing. Upon further reflection I find it both profound and prophetic—an apt description of our postmodern culture with its freewheeling spirituality. What many believe about God is based on personal "spiritual" experience rather than on the revelation of Scripture.[3]

THE CONTRARIAN LIFE OF MOSES	
Age 14	• Forming his youthful personality at the Zenith of a "ME."
Age 40	• Kills the Egyptian taskmaster in the upswing of a "WE." Full of himself. Society doesn't appreciate his heroic efforts in a "WE."
Age 80	• Returns from the desert into the upswing of a "ME." Society wants a leader, but he doesn't feel up to it.
Age 120	• Ego puffed up, Moses defiantly strikes the rock in the upswing of a "WE." Like with the killing of the Egyptian, it doesn't work out for him.

Acknowledgments

No book is written by committee. *Pendulum* certainly wasn't.

But many hands are involved in the extended process of publishing a book, and the authors would like to thank the following people for their contributions in bringing *Pendulum* to readers.

Designer Gary Hespenheide created *Pendulum's* signature look, with assistance from his colleague Randy Miyake.

Leigh Jeffrey, who crafted the first thing that customers will see: our dazzling cover.

Beneath the covers, Robert J. Hughes provided his editorial expertise and marketing support, Kirsten Nelson organized our charts, Jamie Moran synthesized the efforts of our team, Andrea Reindl helped ensure that everyone worked on the same page, so to speak.

Cinde Johnson, for her tireless effort to coordinate between the authors, the author's book team and the publisher.

Michael R. Drew would also like to extend special thanks to his daughter Savannah VaLoy Drew, who lent her hard-pressed father to this project for many, many months of research, writing and design.

The authors would also like to thank Vanguard Press publisher Roger Cooper, Melanie Mitman, Vanguard marketing director, and Christine E. Marra, its editor and design coordinator.

David Hahn and Andrew Palladino from Media Connect get boldface mention for their publicity efforts.

And we'd both like to thank Princess Pennie, who has continued to inspire Roy H. Williams and, by extension, Michael R. Drew, in countless ways.

Notes

CHAPTER ONE
Epiphany

1. "Information Superhighway," Wikipedia, http://en.wikipedia.org/wiki/Information_super_highway.
2. William Strauss and Neil Howe, *Generations: The History of America's Future, 1584 to 2069* (New York: Morrow, 1991).

CHAPTER TWO
"We" versus "Me"

1. David Brooks, "It's Not About You," *The New York Times*, May 30, 2011, http://www.nytimes.com/2011/05/31/opinion/31brooks.html.

CHAPTER THREE
What Defines a Generation?

1. Catherine Colbert, "Marketing to Millennials: Companies Most Admired by the Generation That's Bigger Than the Boomers," Bizmology, March 29, 2011, http://bizmology.hoovers.com/2011/03/29 marketing-to-millennials-companies-most-admired-by-the-generation-thats-bigger-than-the-boomers/.
2. Edward F. Edinger, *Ego and Archetype: Individuation and the Religious Function of the Psyche* (Boston: Shambhala, 1992).
3. Ibid., 37.

CHAPTER FOUR
Duality

1. "Foundation Series," Wikipedia, http://en.wikipedia.org/wiki/Foundation_series.

CHAPTER FIVE
Alpha Voices and the Six-Year Transitionary Window

1. Malcolm Gladwell, *Outliers: The Story of Success* (Boston; Little Brown and Company, 2008), 62.

CHAPTER SIX
The Limits of Predictability

1. Neil Postman, *Technopoly: The Surrender of Culture to Technology* (New York: Knopf, 1992).

CHAPTER SEVEN
1923–1933: First Half of the Upswing into "We"

1. "The Sun Also Rises," Wikipedia, http://en.wikipedia.org/wiki/The_Sun_Also_Rises. Emphasis added.
2. "Albert Schweitzer > Quotes" Good Reads, http://www.goodreads.com/author/quotes/47146.Albert_Schweitzer.
3. Elizabeth Stevenson, *Babbitts and Bohemians: From the Great War to the Great Depression* (New York: Macmillan, 1967), 114.
4. Ibid., 154.
5. Kenneth Bruce, *YOWSAH! YOWSAH! YOWSAH! The Roaring Twenties* (Belmont, CA: Star Publishing Company, 1981), 79.
6. Stevenson, *Babbitts and Bohemians*. "Technology: The Impact of Technology on 1920s Life," Angelfire, http://www.angelfire.com/co/pscst/tech.html.

CHAPTER EIGHT
1933–1943: The Second Half of the Upswing, Reaching the Zenith of "We"

1. Kathleen McLaughlin, "Hecklers Shout Disapproval of Hitler Defender. Berlin Savant Explains Why Books Were Burned," *New York Times,* November 15, 1933.

2. Franklin Delano Roosevelt, "Address of President Roosevelt by Radio, Delivered from the White House at 10 p.m., March 12, 1933," in Amos Kiewe, *FDR's First Fireside Chat: Public Confidence and the Banking Crisis*, 1–6 (College Station: Texas A&M University Press, 2007). Emphasis added.

CHAPTER NINE
Three Thousand Years of "We" and the Origin of Western Society

1. 2 Chronicles 30:26.
2. "Human Rights," Wikipedia, http://en.wikipedia.org/wiki/ Human_rights.
3. 2 Chronicles 36:21–23.
4. "Julius Caesar," Wikipedia, http://en.wikipedia.org/wiki/Julius _Caesar.
5. "Pliny the Younger," Wikipedia, http://en.wikipedia.org/wiki/ Pliny_the_Younger.
6. "Emperor Honorius," Wikipedia, http://en.wikipedia.org/wiki/ Emperor_Honorius.
7. "Winchester College," Wikipedia, http://en.wikipedia.org/wiki/ Winchester_College.
8. Ibid.
9. "Thomas Malory," Wikipedia, http://en.wikipedia.org/wiki/ Thomas_Malory.
10. "John Donne: Meditation XVII, from "Devotions upon Emergent Occasions," 1624, Sublime to the Ridiculous, http://lazydabbler. wordpress.com/2010/03/21/john-donnemeditation-xvii-from -devotions-upon-emergent-occasions/.\11.
11. "Statue of Liberty," Wikipedia, http://en.wikipedia.org/wiki/ Statue_of_Liberty.
12. John Steinbeck, *The Log from the Sea of Cortez* (New York: Penguin, 1995).
13. Ibid., 96.
14. George Bernard Shaw, *Caesar and Cleopatra*, Act III.

CHAPTER TEN

1943–1953: The First Half of the Downswing of "We"

1. John Lahr, The New Yorker, May 9, 2011.

CHAPTER ELEVEN

1953–1963: The Second Half of the Downswing of "We"

1. Charles Baudelaire, "Be Drunk," Poets.org, http://www.poets. org/viewmedia.php/prmMID/16054.
2. "Charles Baudelaire," Wikipedia, http://en.wikipedia.org/wiki/ Charles_Baudelaire.
3. Jack Kerouac, *On the Road.* New York: Penguin, 1999.
4. J. D. Salinger, *The Catcher in the Rye* (Boston: Little, Brown, and Co., 1955), 52, 113, 117.
5. Ellis Amburn, *Subterranean Kerouac: The Hidden Life of Jack Kerouac* (New York: MacMillan, 1999), 13–14.
6. Joseph Lelyveld, *New York Times,* October 22, 1969.
7. "Jack Kerouac," Wikipedia, http://en.wikipedia.org/wiki/ Jack_Kerouac.
8. Karen Schoemer, *Great Pretenders: My Strange Love Affair with '50s Pop Music* (New York: Free Press, 2006) 79.
9. "Albert Schweitzer Quotes," Goodreads, http://www.goodreads .com/author/quotes/47146.Albert_Schweitzer.
10. Anne Morrow Lindbergh, *Gift from the Sea* (New York: Pantheon Books, 1991), ch. 8.

CHAPTER TWELVE

1963–1973: The First Half of the Upswing into "Me"

1. Jaron Lanier,. "Digital Maoism: The Hazards of the New Online Collectivism," *The Edge,* May 29, 2006, http://edge.org/conversation /digital-maoism-the-hazards-of-the-new-online-collectivism. Emphasis added.
2. "Louie Louie," Wikipedia, http://en.wikipedia.org/wiki/ Louie_Louie.

3. Robert Stone, *Prime Green: Remembering the Sixties* (New York: Harper Perennial, 2007), 92.

4. "But Wait! There's More: Book Chronicals Popeil and Ronco Commercials," Transcript of original Vegematic TV Commercial, NPR, June 19, 2003, http://www.npr.org/programs/morning/features/2002/june/ronco/.

5. John Steinbeck, *Paradox and Dream* (1966).

6. "Salem Witch Trials," Wikipedia, http://en.wikipedia.org/wiki/Salem_witch_trials.

7. Hunter S. Thomson, *Fear and Loathing in Las Vegas* (New York: Vintage, 1971)

8. Hunter S. Thompson, *Kingdom of Fear: Loathsome Secrets of a Star-Crossed Child in the Final Days of the American Century,* New York: Simon and Scheuster, 2004.

9. Hunter S. Thompson, "The 'Hashbury' Is the Capital of the Hippies," Byliner, May 1967, http://byliner.com/hunter-s-thompson/stories/the-hashbury-is-the-capital-of-the-hippies.

10. Don McLean, BBC Radio 2 interview, November 4, 1993.

CHAPTER THIRTEEN

1973–1983: The Upswing of "Me" Reaches Its Limit

1. "Breakfast of Champions," Wikipedia, http://en.wikipedia.org/wiki/Breakfast_of_Champions.

CHAPTER FOURTEEN

Three Thousand Years of "Me": A "Me" Is About Big Dreams

1. "Byzantium," Wikipedia, http://en.wikipedia.org/wiki/Byzantium.

2. "Galerius," Wikipedia, http://en.wikipedia.org/wiki/Galerius.

3. "Quran," Wikipedia, http://cn.wikipedia.org/wiki/Quran.

4. Barron carra de Vaux, *Les Penseurs de l'Islam*, vol. 2 (Paris: Paul Geuthner), 213.

5. "Henry I of England," Wikipedia, http://en.wikipedia.org/wiki/
   Henry_I_of_England.
6. John Fines, *Who's Who in the Middle Ages* (New York: Stein and
   Day, 1971), 22.
7. "Pope Julius II," Wikipedia, http://en.wikipedia.org/wiki/
   Pope_Julius_II.
8. Ibid.

CHAPTER FIFTEEN

1983–2003: The Twenty-Year Downswing from "Me"

1. "FrodeVarn's Mazda Miata MX-5 'Supercharged Black & Tan',"
   CarDomain, http://www.cardomain.com/ride/301314/
   1992-mazda-miata-mx-5.
2. William Strauss and Neil Howe, The Fourth Turning—An
   American Prophecy: What the Cycles of History Tell Us About
   America's Next Rendezvous with Destiny (New York: Broadway
   Books, 1997).

CHAPTER SIXTEEN

2003–2023: The Twenty-Year Upswing into "We" *One More Time*

1. "Gigli," Box Office Mojo, http://boxofficemojo.com/
   movies/?id=gigli.htm.
2. "Pirates of the Caribbean: The Curse of the Black Pearl," Box
   Office Mojo, http://boxofficemojo.com/movies/?id=piratesofthe
   caribbean.htm.
3. "Goodreads > Carl Rogers." GoodReads, http://www.goodreads.
   com/author/quotes/1353353.Carl_Rogers.

CHAPTER SEVENTEEN

2013–2023: What Happens Next? A Discussion of Experts

1. Jaron Lanier, *You Are Not a Gadget: A Manifesto* (New York:
   Vintage, 2011).
2. John Steinbeck, *East of Eden* (New York: Penguin, 2002), ch. 13.

3. Gary Rust, "Looking Ahead to 2004," *Southeast Missourian,* December 30, 2003, http://www.semissourian.com/story/127605. html.
4. "Quotes: Human Nature (Non-Religious)," Math.UCLA.edu, http://www.math.ucla.edu/~tao/quotes.html.
5. Society in *Brave New World* is divided into five castes that are designed to fulfill predetermined positions within the social and economic strata of the World State. Fetuses chosen to become members of the highest caste, Alpha, are allowed to develop naturally, whereas fetuses chosen to become members of the lower castes, Beta, Gamma, Delta, and Epsilon are subjected to chemical interference in order to cause arrested development in intelligence and physical growth.
6. "The future is already here—it's just not very evenly distributed." According to Wikipedia, Gibson is reported to have first said this in an interview on *Fresh Air,* National Public Radio, August 31, 1993.

CHAPTER EIGHTEEN
Uses of the Pendulum

1. *Harvard Business Review* (December 1966): 147–157.

CHAPTER NINETEEN
Pendulum in the Bible

1. Numbers 12:3.
2. Spencer Marsh, *God, Man and Archie Bunker* (New York: Bantam Books, 1976), 1.
3. Richard Exely, "Where Have All the Critical Thinkers Gone?" Richard Exely Ministries, July 2, 2009, http://www.richardexley ministries.org/index.cfm?id=7&init_blogid=39.

Index

About Roy H. Williams

Roy H. Williams dropped out of college on the second day, choosing instead to "figure it out" for himself. At age 19, he began asking local business owners, "Have you ever done any advertising that you felt really worked? Tell me about it." After cataloguing their answers, he asked, "Have you ever done any advertising that you thought was brilliant—something you were really excited about— that failed miserably?"

"You only have to ask a few hundred business owners," says Williams, "before it all becomes crystal clear . . . everyone makes the same mistakes for the same reasons. And the things that work brilliantly have common denominators as well. All the answers, of course, are initially counterintuitive. That's why everyone makes the same mistakes. I was given thousands of years of collective experience and the results of more than one hundred million dollars in advertising expenditures . . . *for free.* All I had to do was see the patterns. What a country!"

At 20, Williams began consulting small business owners across America, guiding dozens of them to unprecedented success. Twenty years later, his *Wizard of Ads* trilogy of business books rose to the top of the *New York Times* and *Wall Street Journal* bestseller lists.

Williams continues to consult business owners through his online MondayMorningMemo and his private consulting firm, Roy H. Williams Marketing in Austin, Texas. He currently has 54 *Wizard of Ads* business partners helping grow more than 900 small businesses around the world.

He is also the founder of Wizard Academy, a 501c3 nonprofit business school whose sole objective is to strengthen the small-business backbone of every country on earth. "Profitable companies employ people, give them purpose, and keep them too busy to go to war."

"We teach big things fast," says Williams. "The most recent U.S. census tells us the United States has 5.91 million businesses with fewer than 100 employees. Wizard Academy was built expressly for them." Alumni of Wizard Academy include Nobel Prize-winning scientists, Pulitzer Prize-winning journalists, marketing executives from Fortune 500 companies and "a high percentage of gun slinging entrepreneurs."

Roy Williams lives in Austin, Texas, with Pennie Compton Williams, the girl with whom he fell in love at the age of 14. They have two adult sons and two young grandsons.

About Michael R. Drew

Michael R. Drew has been marketing books for his entire career. He's become the world's most successful book promoter, having helped launch nearly 75 books onto best-seller lists, many of them number-one titles. Beyond merely helping authors' books to sell well, Michael has benefited from these writers' insights into social trends. He himself has observed up-close the shifting dynamics of society— as with his work on *Pendulum—and has seen firsthand the rapid and long-term changes in the publishing industry and how content reaches today's varied audiences.*

Michael honed his skills at such respected publishers as Bard Press, Entrepreneur Magazine, Longstreet Press and Thomas Nelson Publishers, among others. He has mastered the intricacies of publishing and, in adapting to today's fast-evolving industry, Michael founded Promote a Book to work directly with writers to help them spread their message.

Michael has also helped writers and authors build upon an essential component of continuing success, creating a platform for their writing and their message so that they can expand their audience and adapt to social shifts. Through Michael's skills in website creation, his strengths as a speaker, his career coaching and in his innovative use of personas to intensify the effectiveness of all sorts of writing, Michael has been a force in the creation of a new generation of thought leaders. He has helped them to become even more effective entrepreneurs who nourish today's idea-hungry marketplace.

And as shifts in society continue, Michael has expanded Promote A Book's services to include consulting and planning on everything from Internet distribution and website-building to video creation, book trailers, podcasting and more.

"Buy this book now! Roy H. Williams and Michael R. Drew reveal great reasons for social change based on compelling cultural shifts—and it's all here in lively, opinionated prose."

—**Mark Thompson, Co-author of the Best-selling Books**
Now, Build a Great Business** and **Success Built to Last

"Pendulum is quite an eye-opener. I had no idea that the generational shifts in society were so important throughout history. I felt instantly empowered by the uncommon truths that Roy H. Williams and Michael R. Drew have given me in their engaging book, especially in understanding the marketplace today—and tomorrow. I now feel I've got an edge in how to connect effectively with others and lead my business organization to the top."

—**Laura Silva Quesada, President, Silva Method International**

"85% of the planet is connected with mobile phones or the Internet, but we still need to figure out what people like or don't like. Thanks to *Pendulum* we do. Roy H. Williams and Michael R. Drew have discovered that people don't change so much but their attitudes and outlooks do! These guys show how society shifts every generation—and why that matters. *Pendulum* is a great read and a great resource for all marketers and networkers."

—**Mike Koenigs, Creator of Traffic Geyser and Instant Customer**

"Roy H. Williams & Michael R. Drew's *Pendulum* is a remarkable book and an enlightening idea. It has helped me rethink the way I brand and market my business and myself. We have introduced his concepts to every layer of our company and his ideas have helped us add new perspectives and layers of sophistication to the way we build online websites and run our business."

—**Vishen Lakhiani, Founder & CEO, MindValley.com**

"This book reveals a no-hype and no-nonsense perspective on how human history shows us a predictable future in remarkably accurate 40-year cycles—if we lift our blindfolds. Roy and Michael demonstrate that our future (and our children's future) will either be big and bright, OR dark and gloomy—we get to choose!"

—**Alex Mandossian, CEO and Founder, MarketingOnline.com**

"As someone who believes strongly in the laws of attraction, I look for ways in which people can connect. *Pendulum* provides not only the framework for understanding society today and tomorrow, but also the background for how we got here (and why we're getting there). It's an essential read for any entrepreneur, marketer or creative thinker who wants to connect with how people think."

—Glen Ledwell, CEO, mindmovies.com

"If you're a business owner or entrepreneur, you already know there's a shift happening in the economy and the business world—but you may not clearly understand why it's occurring. This book will not only explain it, but will show you specifically how to adapt to this massive change and ride the wave instead of being destroyed by it. We've retooled and reoriented our core business as a direct result of what you're about to learn, and the results have been astounding. Engagement and authenticity are truly the new currency of business, and this book will allow you incorporate them successfully into your organization."

—Greg Habstritt, President & Founder SimpleWealth.com

"If you really want to build a mega-successful business, you must be able to always stay ahead of the curve. It's not an option! And by reading this book, understanding the Pendulum "principles", and putting it into practice—you will understand how to meet your customers exactly where you are. And that, my friend, is where the millions (and billions) are made!"

—Ryan Lee, Entrepreneur, Author, Coach, www.ryanlee.com

"Society changes all the time, yet keeps coming back to certain opposite principles: civic-mindedness or individualism. *Pendulum* shows why—and how anyone, from marketers to entrepreneurs, can navigate these shifts for greater impact on profits, people and planet. Roy H. Williams and Michael R. Drew have parsed the historical record and given us an entertaining and useful look at where we are as a culture, and where we're going."

—Jim Kwik, *The Art of WARMTH*

"In their exciting new book, *Pendulum,* Roy H. Williams and Michael R. Drew have done an amazing job of revealing what motivates behavior. The authors share how society shifts every generation and why that's important to understand for today's business success. My motto for many years has been, "Relationships first, business second." For businesses to succeed in today's highly-connected world, you must understand what motivates people to engage, to refer their friends, and ultimately to make purchases. Get ready for a deep dive into today's culture and tomorrow's challenges; *Pendulum* will give you the tools you need to build your online network and motivate prospects to action."

—Mari Smith, Social Media Expert and Trainer, Author of the
best-seller, *The New Relationship Marketing*

"There's so much humor and wisdom and insight in *Pendulum!* Roy H. Williams and Michael R. Drew show us why we are thinking the way we do now—and they know this because they've closely studied the last 3,000 years of history. I learned so much more about effective communicating thanks to *Pendulum,* and anyone who wants to understand how we look at the world should use this book. It's a terrific read and a great resource."

—MaryEllen Tribby, Founder and CEO of WorkingMomsOnly.com, and Co-author of the
Best-selling Book, *Changing the Channel: 12 Easy Ways to Make Millions For Your Business*

"Move your pendulum to "dollar sign as your true north" within the first pages of this remarkable book. It's filled with insight and great tools for understanding the world. Michael R. Drew's principles have created more wealth, more best-selling books and more success in general than anyone alive, and his spirit and Roy H. Williams' wisdom shine in the pages of *Pendulum,* so everyone can benefit from their remarkable work."

—Berny Dohrmann, Founder, CEOSpaceInternational.com,
Author, Radio-show Host, Movie Producer

"*Pendulum* is an incredible look into what's "coming next" and how we can almost predict the future. Roy H. Williams and Michael R. Drew have studied how society has functioned through all of civilization to explain where we are now, and what's going to happen to us over the next 40 years and beyond. *Pendulum* is thought-provoking and just a little bit scary. A must read!"

—Amish Shah, Chief Product Officer of Bitzio, Inc, Founder of DigiSpace Solutions

"The first time I saw Michael R. Drew deliver *Pendulum,* he was following the Dalia Lama, and his presentation and ideas wowed the crowd as much as His Holiness did. Since then, what I learned from him and his ideas in *Pendulum* has shifted the way we work with and consult with our clients, and has been integral in helping my company grow to where it is today."

—Craig Handley, CEO, Listen Up Espanol, #1 in Business Products and Services INC 500

"I'm delighted *Pendulum* is now a book! I've seen Michael R. Drew's full Pendulum presentation twice and each time I've been amazed, thrilled and sure that I've got the inside track to the rhythm of time, history, human nature and more. Roy H. Williams and Michael R. Drew have done an amazing job of pointing the way. I'm so grateful I learned about this during a "We" time, especially since I feel the most connection with the collective in general."

—Kim Coles, Award-winning Actress, Speaker and Entrepreneur

"Michael R. Drew and Roy H. Williams' understanding of mass social psychology and trends is scarily spot on. They show a deep understanding of character and human behavior. *Pendulum* will change how marketers do business. Anybody who doesn't get ahead of the pendulum will find themselves on the wrong end of it. Impressive and surprising."

—Eric Michael Collins, CEO, Fast Attract

"The world we live in today is changing dramatically. Reading *Pendulum* is like having a master class in consumer marketing. Roy H. Williams and Michael R. Drew have handed business owners a valuable gift—a blueprint for how to speak to today's consumers in a language and style that they'll respond to. Use it and profit. Ignore it at your peril."

—Andrew Lock, Marketing Expert, and Presenter of the
Hit WebTV show, "Help! My Business Sucks!"

"I loved *Pendulum*. Roy H. Williams and Michael R. Drew have given us remarkable tools to understand what's going on all around us today. If you're wondering why we think the way we do in at any time, any decade, *Pendulum* explains why. It's all about generational shifts—and it's been like that for thousands of years. Who knew? I'll be using *Pendulum* again and again to get a bead on society."

—Chris Ryan, Senior Editor, *NewsWire*

"The world has gone 'bland'. Repackaged, tired concepts everywhere. Until now! *Pendulum* excites, stimulates and inspires. Fresh big picture thinking that can translate into major business success when put to use."

—Patrick Gentempo, Jr., D.C., CEO, Action Potential Holdings, LLC

Pendulum is a game changer for anyone that is serious about success! Michael has unlocked the code to help you understand what winning looks like from the inside! It is a must read!

—Bill Walsh "America's Business Expert"

"*Pendulum* may be the most important book you read all year. This is not a book about business, but one about how culture has changed, which will dramatically alter the way you must do business. It will open your eyes to exactly what is happening in the world today and how your business must respond."

—Eric Rhoads, Publisher, *Radio Ink*

"We've all heard how history repeats. Now we know why. We humans swing from selfish to social every generation or so, and civilization swings with us. In their surprising, insightful and witty new book, *Pendulum,* Roy H. Williams and Michael R. Drew explain us to us. They explore the real reasons behind some of civilization's greatest advances—and retreats. They show us why we repeat ourselves—but they also give us the tools that might prevent future catastrophes. And who knew that pop music said so much about our social selves?"

—Robert J. Hughes, Former *Wall Street Journal* reporter and
Author of the Novel, *Late and Soon*

"A must read as Michael R. Drew in *Pendulum* cracks the code on life's mystery as to why history repeats itself, giving us the crystal ball to see the future in advance to position ourselves to live passionate, purposeful, productive and prosperous lives in a rapidly and dramatically changing world. Thank you, Michael, for the gift."

—Jeffrey Spencer, D.C., Author, *Turn It Up, How To Perform At Your Best For A Lifetime*

"Imagine thousands of seemingly random societal transformations suddenly crystalized into one straight-forward explanation. This book not only explains why we've seen so many shifts in thought, but shows you how to predict what's next. This book is a powerful shortcut to anticipating what marketing messages will make customers want to buy."

—Robert Skrob, Author of Official Get Rich Guide to Information Marketing

"A big challenge in society is how we work together—and how we see each other.
Pendulum shows us not only how, but why. Roy H. Williams and Michael R. Drew take us through profound shifts in society over the course of our civilization and explain several key distinctions that are absolutely critical to your overall success and happiness. *Pendulum* is a must read for all entrepreneurs and for anyone who wants to understand the world around us."

—Manny Goldman, Founder and CEO, Real Growth Worldwide,
Author, *The Power of Personal Growth*

"Ever wanted a time machine so you can leap into the future to see what will happen? That time machine is here, now in the book *Pendulum* by Roy H. Williams and Michael R. Drew. Roy and Michael have written a thoroughly researched book that will help you understand the impact on you, your family and your business from the cultural tsunami of change that is engulfing Western culture. As clear and precise as a German-made metronome, *Pendulum* traces an 80-year predictable pattern of societal and cultural change back through time and uses this knowledge to reliably forecast what's ahead. My company is using the knowledge we've gained from *Pendulum* to position ourselves to successfully navigate this sea-change. You should, too."

—Sid Lloyd, President & CEO, Full Plate Diet (Ardmore Institute of Health)

"*Pendulum* feeds my unyielding passion for understanding natural patterns in technology, business, politics and society. Roy H. Williams and Michael R. Drew provide priceless insight into what's happening now and how the future will unfold, by chronicling our connection to the ebbs and flows of western society over the past 3,000 years. Their findings have forever changed my perspective on how I approach mass communication."

—Hugh Stewart, Author of *The Magic of High Quality Questions* and *How I Beat Wal-Mart*

"Lone rangers and gurus are out. Contributors and selflessness are in. Roy H. Williams and Michael R. Drew make an incredibly powerful case for why every individual and organization needs to move to a We mindset. Societal's pendulum is swinging. This book will help you leverage its momentum."

—Stephen Shapiro, Author, *Best Practices Are Stupid*

"Roy H. Williams sees things that no one else can: finding connections between things that seem utterly unrelated. I am sure he could find the connections between Yoga and Pepper Spray and from it form profitable strategies for business leaders. This time he has teamed with Michael R. Drew, and together they have discovered a cycle of human behavior repeating itself for at least 3000 years. *Pendulum* is a must read for anyone wanting to know what's next and why."

—At age 31, Mark Fox was the youngest person with the title of Chief Engineer on the Space Shuttle Program.

"Human potential is limitless, but society keeps coming back to a "me" or "we" focus every generation or so. That affects how we look at the world, and how we work with each other.

Pendulum details not only how such cultural shifts have profound impacts on business and interpersonal relationships, but how you can learn to work within each swing of the pendulum, each cycle of history. Michael R. Drew and Roy H. Williams have uncovered the way to target success no matter where society is today or in the future."

—Shellie Hunt, Founder/CEO, Success Is By Design

"It's all about connections, and *Pendulum* shows us why. What was true 3,000 years ago is truer today—Roy H. Williams and Michael R. Drew have combed through history's social shifts and found how each generation looks at the world a little differently, and why that's important to everyone, from marketers to writers to politicians to entrepreneurs. *Pendulum* will rock your world. It rocked mine."

—David Bullock, Social Media Expert and Co-author of the Best-selling Book *Barack 2.0*

"I love *Pendulum*. It articulates clearly the evolution of people's motivations that I've witnessed in my classrooms over the past 20-plus years. Even better than contextualizing the past, *Pendulum* gives us a glimpse into the future and guides us as to what we can do about it in our lives and businesses. Thanks to Roy H. Williams and Michael R. Drew for confirming what I intuitively felt, but could not clearly articulate."

—Jay Fiset, Entrepreneur, Speaker, Author of the Best Seller,
Reframe Your Blame and Founder of The Creator's Code

"Roy H. Williams and Michael R. Drew have unlocked the code as to why we do what we do! In *Pendulum,* they uncovered why society changes every 40 years or so, and why that's important to any marketer or entrepreneur. In fact, to everyone. I learned so much from *Pendulum*. It's so much more then marketing; it will change the way you look at the world."

—Brad Powers, CMO, Aspen University

"For anyone who wants to move ahead in business development or networking, *Pendulum* has the goods. Roy H. Williams and Michael R. Williams show how society keeps changing—and returning to what it used to be. For marketers it's golden information: these guys have discovered why we think the way we do at any given period. Fantastic stuff!"

—David Gonzalez, Founder, Velvet Rope Joint Ventures

"Looking back to determine trends that can be projected forward is a critical skill to see ahead and plan. Michael's brilliant introduction of this concept has enabled my clients and me to prepare for the next decade . . . not just the next year. Knowing our history also helps identify the characteristics of the leaders who will emerge. *Pendulum* is critical-thinking material for the critical thinker who wants to see the wave coming before it gets here."

—**Dr. Steve Hoffman, Discover Wellness, Inc., MC2 & Mastery Coaching, 2ndCousin, Inc. Media & Marketing**

"As society swirls around us, many of us wonder how to make things happen for ourselves. *Pendulum* gives us the tools to understand where we are in society and how to capitalize on it. Roy H. Williams and Michael R. Drew are inspired guides to history's social shifts. Their profound insights will help you identify opportunities and make you a better businessperson."

—**Sean Roach, CEO and Founder of Idea Catapult, Inc., Author of *Get Off Your Duff* and *Make Your Own Damn Cheese!***

"For me, as a professor of philosophy and an entrepreneur, *Pendulum* is my chaperon. It reveals a generation's trajectory and how that affects my ability to engage both my students and clients. This exploration of generational heroes and villains, of fads and fashion, of what sells and what does not, makes for a brilliant piece of work! Roy H. Williams and Michael R. Drew take history and turn it into a compelling read and a persuasive argument for listening to social patterns—and an opportunity to act on the challenges ahead. *Pendulum* is a must read. I've recommended to all of my colleagues."

—**Ralph J. Argen III, PhD, Coherence First**

"Why is it we sometimes think others know best and at other times we're sure we know what's what? *Pendulum* explains it all. Roy H. Williams and Michael R. Drew show us how society's shifts affect how we look at the world. And this has been happening throughout history and music in particular. An awesome look at why we do what we do, why we think as we do, and what tomorrow may bring. It has helped me in writing music that speaks to our culture now and where we are going. My album, "Awake and Arise" was written in mind with the principles that this book reveals."

—**Jhonny K, Musician, Entrepreneur, Humanitarian**

"*Pendulum* explains why society swings back and forth every 40 years. You can either ride this fact to success, or fight an uphill battle pushing against it. But who wants to push against it? Grab this book now."

—**Mahesh Grossman, President of AuthorsTeam.com and**
Author of ***Write a Book Without Lifting a Finger***

"*Pendulum* is a fascinating look at society and success and brilliantly reveals a solid architecture that most would never know existed. You've absolutely got to check this book out."

—**Nick Nanton, Esq., Emmy Award Winning Director and Top Agent to Celebrity Experts**

"*Pendulum* is the business resource for our generation. This book needs to be absorbed, applied and read again and again. The concepts that Michael R. Drew and Roy H. Williams introduce are a combination of Warren Buffett and H.G. Wells that can positively impact every decision you make in your business and your life. And it's all based on historical, proven data! Michael and Roy deliver the information in a straight-forward manner, so that we can apply concepts that probably belong in a quantum physics lesson! *Pendulum* is going right beside *Freakonomics* on the "Must Read Again" shelf in my resource library."

—**Ron Edgar – CEO, Sales Pitbull Consulting Group**

"How you communicate with others, how you market yourself and your ideas are so important —but who knows what will work or not? Roy H. Williams and Michael R. Drew do: In their exciting new book *Pendulum,* they reveal the way society works, and why we like what we do when we do. They've combed history to find how generations shift, and what that means to you. This book is essential to the success of any marketer or entrepreneur. Don't just read it. Study it, consume it and implement it. These fundamentals will take your business to a whole new level."

—**Jeff Schneider, Founder & CEO, MarketingNinjas.com**

"*Pendulum* has it all: biblical references, historical insights and pop-music commentary! This is a terrific look at society changes, both through its major players and artists, and through the subtle shifts of society every generation or so. It made me realize how we got where we are. And also how history keeps repeating itself! Thought-provoking and essential—*Pendulum* delivers."

—**Kari Dunlop, Founder, President, Glinda Girls, The Business of Bliss**

"I'm so glad the Pendulum presentation is finally in book form. There is just so much great intelligence that when presented live you simply can't absorb it fully. If you have any interest at all in where the world is headed, how our culture is evolving or what tomorrow's consumers will be thinking—if you have a pulse in other words—Michael and Roy give advanced insights that are absolutely priceless! Spooky accuracy and impact would be the best way to describe it."

—Jay Niblick, Founder of Innermetrix International, and
Author of the Best-selling book, *What's Your Genius?*

"Highlighting examples from literature, business and world history, Roy H. Williams and Michael R. Drew offer a bird's eye view of the pulsing 'heartbeat of society.' *Pendulum* reveals our cultural perspective—crucial insight to transform how we build businesses, create relationships and define our personal and collective success."

—Mindie Kniss, Creator of RestartYourHeart.com and Award-winning Humanitarian

"*Pendulum* is amazing—I couldn't put it down. Roy H. Williams and Michael R. Drew provide insights into society that will absolutely transform the way I do business. A must-read: smart, provocative, funny and essential."

—Brad Axelrad, Consultant, Speaker and Internet Entrepreneur

"In *Pendulum,* Roy H. Williams and Michael R. Drew do a masterful job of defining the shifts in history that have defined each era and connects that comprehensive compilation of data to the relevance for current day leaders. I do not know how anyone who aspires to be a leader can be successful without reading *Pendulum.* Though the data is extensive, the book is compelling. I found it easy to read, yet hard to put down. This is a MUST READ."

—Hugh Ballou, The Transformational Leadership Strategist

"One of the interesting principles of a pendulum is that its period doesn't change; it swings just as fast with a bowling ball at the end as it does with an elephant attached. This book clearly demonstrates that our collective cultural pendulum swings with an 80-year period, regardless of the weight of historical events. Now, as we swing out of the "Me" and prepare for the coming "We," it's good to have some guidance we can count on, so that our way of communicating can more effective and engaging. For many, the pendulum will overtake them like a wrecking ball. For others it will serve as a metronome tapping out the rhythms of our generational shifts. This work will help you avoid the ball."

—Brian Massey, Conversion Scientist, Author and Speaker